D0140473

TABLE OF CONTENTS

Top 20 Test Taking Tips

1. Carefully follow all the test registration procedures
2. Know the test directions, duration, topics, question types, how many questions
3. Setup a flexible study schedule at least 3-4 weeks before test day
4. Study during the time of day you are most alert, relaxed, and stress free
5. Maximize your learning style; visual learner use visual study aids, auditory learner use auditory study aids
6. Focus on your weakest knowledge base
7. Find a study partner to review with and help clarify questions
8. Practice, practice, practice
9. Get a good night's sleep; don't try to cram the night before the test
10. Eat a well balanced meal
11. Know the exact physical location of the testing site; drive the route to the site prior to test day
12. Bring a set of ear plugs; the testing center could be noisy
13. Wear comfortable, loose fitting, layered clothing to the testing center; prepare for it to be either cold or hot during the test
14. Bring at least 2 current forms of ID to the testing center
15. Arrive to the test early; be prepared to wait and be patient
16. Eliminate the obviously wrong answer choices, then guess the first remaining choice
17. Pace yourself; don't rush, but keep working and move on if you get stuck
18. Maintain a positive attitude even if the test is going poorly
19. Keep your first answer unless you are positive it is wrong
20. Check your work, don't make a careless mistake

United States Government

The Articles of Confederation

The very first constitution in the history of the United States was the Articles of Confederation. The Articles of Confederation served as a plan for the government of the United States and was created on the principles that were defended during the Revolutionary War. However, the Articles of Confederation contained weaknesses. Specifically, the Articles of Confederation did not assign the power to create and collect taxes, did not assign power to oversee trade, and it created a relatively weak executive power without the ability to enforce legislation. The greatest fault of the Articles of Confederation was that it did not originate with the people, but rather power was vested in the states to avoid a central government authority. Under the Articles of Confederation, every state could collect its own taxes, issue currency, and maintain its own militia, creating inefficiencies in the national government. The national government was primarily responsible for foreign policy and treaties. The Articles of Confederation provides learning opportunities and was a stepping stone in creating the Constitution.

U.S. Constitution

The U.S. Constitution represents the highest law within the United States. It was the successor of the Articles of Confederation and was finished in 1787, adopted by the Constitutional Convention in Philadelphia, and subsequently ratified by the thirteen original states. The U.S. Constitution established a federal union of sovereign states, as well as a federal government to oversee the union. The U.S. Constitution went into effect in 1789 and has been a model for constitutions created within other nations. The Fourteenth Amendment of the Constitution provides all United States citizens with equal protection under the Constitution. The judiciary branch of the federal government has the power to review the constitutionality of laws passed in the United States and can strike down laws if they are determined to be unconstitutional. The Fifth Article of the Constitution addresses how Congress may propose Constitutional amendments. In addition, a convention consisting of at least two thirds of the states can propose Constitutional amendments. Amendments must be ratified before they become part of the Constitution.

There are a number of documents that influenced the writing of the United States Constitution. These include the Magna Carta, which was written in 1215 A.D. and represented the English liberty charter. In addition, the Mayflower Compact was influential; it was written in 1620 by the first settlers in the New England colony. The Virginia Declaration of Rights was written in 1776 and served as a prototype for other state constitutions and for the Bill of Rights. The Declaration of Independence was also adopted in 1776 and was influential in the writing of the Constitution. The Articles of Confederation was adopted in 1781 and served as the first constitution for the original thirteen states following the American Revolution. The Federalist Papers also served as an influence for the drafters of the U.S. Constitution; they were published in newspapers to encourage ratification of the Constitution, which was ratified in 1788.

The U.S. Constitution was written with the influence of international sources and factors. While a number of the concepts represented in the U.S. Constitution were unique, others were taken from classical political theories and from the British model of mixed government. Specifically, the U.S. Constitution was influenced by sections of the Magna Carta, which was written in the year 1215. Another influential document in the drafting of the U.S. Constitution included the English Bill of Rights, which was established in 1689. Specifically, as in the English Bill of Rights, the U.S. Constitution mandates a trial by jury, includes the right to bear arms, and bans the application of extreme bail amounts and cruel and unusual punishments. Many of the rights provided by the Magna Carta and the 1689 English Bill of Rights were indoctrinated in state laws and in the Virginia Declaration of Rights, and subsequently were indoctrinated in the Bill of Rights and the U.S. Constitution.

Originalism

The term originalism encompasses a set of theories regarding constitutional interpretation. People who are proponents of originalism believe that the meaning of the Constitution does not evolve, but is fixed and should be followed and upheld by Judges. Originalism as a form of constitutional interpretation is often favored by individuals who associate themselves with conservative political ideals in the United States. There are numerous theories that fall under the category of originalism. These theories include original intent, which is the opinion that Constitutional interpretation should agree with the originally intended meaning of the people who wrote and ratified the Constitution. A second theory is original understanding, which represents the view that people interpreting the Constitution should seek evidence of what the people who drafted the Constitution understood the Constitution to mean. The third and most

followed originalist theory is original meaning, which is the opinion that interpretation of the Constitution should be founded on what the meaning of the words would have been at the time the Constitution was ratified.

Judicial Activism

Judicial activism is a form of constitutional interpretation in which judicial decisions do not adhere to precedent or extend beyond the limits of conventional law. In reality, any ruling which does not fall within the limits of conventional expectations could be construed as an example of judicial activism. Judges are sometimes accused of judicial activism regardless of their political affiliations and views and regardless of their philosophies regarding judicial interpretation. Critics of judicial activism are concerned that judges who make decisions based on their personal beliefs are not interpreting laws on sound principles. In the U.S., the accusation of judicial activism often carries a negative connotation and refers to decisions that are made to further the interests of specific social or political goals. Specific acts that are associated with judicial activism in the U.S. include the declaration that a law is unconstitutional when it is not; supporting a law that is unconstitutional; overturning judicial precedent; and ruling against the words or intent of laws or the Constitution.

Strict Constructionism

Strict constructionism is a form of judicial interpretation restricting judicial interpretation to the literal meaning of the words and phrases found in laws. Strict constructionism does not allow for other sources to be used or for assumptions to be made about the meaning of the laws beyond the literal words and phrases. Individuals who are proponents of strict constructionism only read text that is explicitly pertinent, and do not permit legislative intent or metaphysical ideas to influence their interpretation. People who support strict constructionism believe that if a legislative body desires to enact a law, its members are knowledgeable about how to draft it and pass it in the words that express their exact intent and meaning and that therefore the judiciary should not be responsible for reconstructing what the intent of the legislative body was.

The Living Constitution

The term Living Constitution is often used to describe the capacity of Congress or of the states to make amendments to the United States Constitution. Specifically, it refers to the process of how amendments can be made that is stated in Article Five of the Constitution. The term Living Constitution is also often applied to characterize how the interpretation of a number of sections within the Constitution has evolved with the application of the Constitution to real world cases throughout the history of the United States since the Constitution was adopted.

Prudentialism

There exist three prudential standing principles, which means that they were judicially created. Congress can override prudential standing principles by passing a statute. The thee prudential standing principles are Prohibition of Third Party Standing, Prohibition of Generalized Grievances, and the Zone of Interest Test. Prohibition of Third Party Standing requires that individuals can only declare their own rights and cannot declare the rights of a third party not before a court. Prohibition of Generalized Grievances requires that a plaintiff cannot sue if an

injury is broadly shared in a similar way with a large number of individuals. The Zone of Interest Test is divided into two tests that are applied by the U.S. Supreme Court. The first is the Zone of Injury, in which the an injury is the type of injury that Congress expected would be covered by the statute. The second is the Zone of Interests, in which the individual is within the zone of interest covered by the statute or by the Constitution.

Textualism

The theory of textualism is a form of constitutional and statutory interpretation. Specifically, proponents of textualism argue that the literal meaning of the Constitution or of a statute should guide the interpretation of the Constitution or of the statute. Individuals who support textualism do not believe that non-textual resources should be used to interpret the Constitution or statutes, such as the legislative intent that was meant when the law was passed, the issue that the law was meant to address or fix, or the important questions of the judge and impartiality of the law.

Governing Principles of the Constitution

The governing principles of the United State Constitution include the principle of popular sovereignty, which is associated with a system of government is created by the people, for the people. Other governing principles of the United State Constitution include the rule of law, the Supreme Court, judicial review, the separation of powers, and the system of checks and balances. In addition, the governing principle of federalism guided the formulation of the United States Constitution, allowing for sharing of power between the federal government and the states. The governing principles of the Constitution also included individual rights, which are embodied in the Bill of Rights.

Bill of Rights

The Bill of Rights includes the first ten amendments to the Constitution. These amendments were proposed to the states by the first Congress of the United States of America as a means to protect personal and civil liberties. The Bill of Rights was originally composed of twelve amendments, which were proposed by Congress on September 25, 1789. In 1791, the group of ten amendments that comprise what is known as the Bill of Rights was ratified by the states. These amendments became part of the Constitution of the United States.

Constitutional Amendments

The process for making amendments to the U.S. Constitution are outlined in Article Five of the Constitution. Amendments can be proposed by either two thirds of both chambers of the United States Congress or by a convention of at least two thirds of the legislatures of the states. Before an amendment can be included in the Constitution, it must be ratified by three fourths of the legislatures of the states, or by three fourths of special conventions that have been assembled in each of the states for the purpose of ratifying the Constitutional amendment. The President of the United States plays no official part in the process of making constitutional amendments. To date, twenty-seven amendments have been ratified and included in the Constitution.

Amendments I-V

The First Amendment protects the five most important civil liberties of citizens of the United States. These civil liberties include the freedom of religion, the freedom of speech, the freedom of the press, the right of assembly, and the freedom to petition. The Second Amendment protects the right to bear arms. The Third Amendment protects the right of citizens not to have troops placed in their private homes. The Fourth Amendment protects citizens against search and seizure of their private homes without a warrant. The Fifth Amendment pertains to the rights of an accused person and protects the right to a trial, the right not to be tried twice for the same crime (double jeopardy), and the right against self incrimination. The Fifth Amendment also protects the right of citizens against the taking of their private property without just compensation.

Amendments VI-X

The Sixth Amendment, like the Fifth Amendment, pertains to the rights of an accused person and protects the right to a speedy trial. The Seventh Amendment protects the right to a jury trial in civil cases. The Eighth Amendment places limitations on bail fines and protects against cruel and unusual punishment. The Ninth Amendment protects the rights of citizens that are not specifically identified in the Constitution and states that such rights shall be respected by the federal government. The Tenth Amendment states that certain powers are retained by the states and by the people.

The Reconstruction Amendments

The Thirteenth, Fourteenth and Fifteenth Amendments are known as the Reconstruction Amendments. They are grouped together in this manner because they were passed during the Reconstruction period following the Civil War. They were drafted with the purpose of abolishing slavery, preventing slavery under other names, and extending rights to all citizens of the United States, regardless of race or color. Specifically, the Thirteenth Amendment, which was ratified in 1865, abolished slavery in the United States. The Fourteenth Amendment, which was ratified in 1868, established limitations on states such that no state may deny any citizen equal protection under the laws. The Fifteenth Amendment, which was ratified in 1870, established the right of citizens to vote regardless of race or color.

The 19th Amendment

The Nineteenth Amendment gave women the right to vote. This amendment was proposed on June 4, 1919 and was ratified on August 18, 1920. An amendment to give women the right to vote was first introduced in Congress in 1878, but it failed to pass. For the next four decades, the amendment was reintroduced in every session of Congress but was defeated each time. The involvement of women in the war effort during World War II spawned increased support for women's suffrage. Finally, in 1918, the House of Representatives approved the amendment to grant women suffrage, but the Senate defeated it. In 1919, the Senate also passed the amendment and sent it to the states for approval, where it was ratified in 1920.

The 25th Amendment

If the Presidency is vacated, the Vice President becomes President. If the Vice Presidency is vacated, the President nominates a Vice President, who must be approved by a majority vote in Congress. If the President informs Congress that he is unable to execute the powers and duties of the Presidency, the Vice President assumes the Presidency until the President informs Congress that he is able to return to office. Similarly, the Vice President will assume the Presidency if

the Vice President and a majority of the Cabinet inform Congress that the President is unable to serve as President, and the President may resume office if he informs Congress that he is able to do so. The Vice President and the Cabinet can counter the President's assertion that he is able to resume office and by a two thirds vote within Congress the Vice President will continue to act as President.

Marbury vs. Madison

Marbury vs. Madison was an 1803 Supreme Court case that established a standard for the constitutional power of the Supreme Court to carry out judicial review of Federal statutes. The Supreme Court decided that it had the power to invalidate a statute which it found to be in violation of the Constitution. The case set the judicial branch as an equal counterpart to the other two branches of the United States federal government. Specifically, Marbury v. Madison was the inaugural case during which the United States Supreme Court used the power of judicial review.

The Dred Scott Case

Dred Scott versus Sandford was an 1857 Supreme Court case that is also referred to as the Dred Scott Case. Dred Scott was a slave who was brought to Illinois, which was a free state, followed by Minnesota, which was a free territory, and finally to Missouri, which was a slave state. When his first master passed away Scott sued for his freedom. A Missouri lower court granted his freedom initially, but it was revoked by the Missouri Supreme Court. At the same time Scott brought his case before a federal court, where he also lost. He then appealed the case to the U.S. Supreme Court, which ruled that blacks, whether free or not, could never be granted U.S. citizenship.

- 9 -

Civil Rights Act of 1871

The Civil Rights Act of 1871 was a statue passed following the Civil War. It was comprised of the 1870 Force Act and the 1871 Ku Klux Klan Act. It was passed primarily with the intention of protecting southern blacks from the Ku Klux Klan. Since it was passed in 1871, the statute has only undergone small changes. It has however, been interpreted widely by the courts. In 1882 some parts of the Civil Rights Act of 1871 were found unconstitutional, but the Force Act and the Klan Act continued to be applied in civil rights cases in subsequent years.

Plessy vs. Ferguson

Plessy vs. Ferguson was an 1896 Supreme Court case. The case resulted in the decision that de jure racial segregation in public facilities was legal in the United States, and permitted states to restrict blacks from using public facilities. The case originated when, in 1890, a black man named Homer Plessy decided to challenge a Louisiana law that segregated blacks and whites on trains by sitting in the white section of a train. Plessy was convicted of breaking the law in a Louisiana court, and the case was appealed to the U.S. Supreme Court, where the Supreme Court upheld the Louisiana decision. The case established the legality of the doctrine of separate but equal, thereby allowing racial segregation. The decision was later overturned by Brown versus the Board of Education of Topeka.

The Fair Employment Act

The Fair Employment Act was signed by President Franklin Roosevelt in 1941. The purpose of the act was to ban racial discrimination in industries related to national defense and represented the very first federal law to ban discrimination in employment. The Fair Employment Act mandated that all federal government agencies and departments concerned with national defense, as well as private defense contractors, guaranteed that professional training would be conducted without discrimination based on race, creed, color, or national origin. The Fair Employment Act was followed by Title VII of the 1964 Civil Rights Act, which banned discrimination by private employers, and by Executive Order 11246 in 1965, which concerned federal contractors and subcontractors.

Presidential Succession Act of 1947

The Presidential Succession Act of 1947 established that if both the President and the Vice President are unable to execute the powers and perform the duties of the Presidency, the position will be assumed by the Speaker of the House, followed by the President pro tempore of the Senate, and then the Cabinet members in the following order: Secretary of State; Secretary of the Treasury; Secretary of Defense; Attorney General; Secretary of the Interior; Secretary of Agriculture; Secretary of Commerce; Secretary of Labor; Secretary of Health and Human Services; Secretary of Housing and Urban Development; Secretary of Transportation; Secretary of Energy; Secretary of Education; Secretary of Veterans Affairs; and Secretary of Homeland Security.

Brown vs. Board of Education

Brown versus the Board of Education of Topeka was a Supreme Court case that was decided in 1954. The case made it illegal for racial segregation to exist within public education facilities. This decision was based on the finding that separate but equal public educational facilities would not provide black and white students with the same standard of facilities. The case originated in 1951, when a lawsuit was filed by Topeka parents, who were recruited by the NAACP, against the Board of Education of the City of Topeka, Kansas in a U.S. District Court. The parents, one of whom was named Oliver Brown, wanted the Topeka Board of Education to eliminate racial segregation. The District Court agreed that segregation had negative effects, but did not force the schools to desegregate because it found that black and white school facilities in the District were generally equal in standards. The case was appealed to the Supreme Court, where the finding was that separate educational facilities are unequal.

Bolling vs. Sharpe

Bolling vs. Sharpe was a 1954 Supreme Court case. Like Brown v. Board of Education, this case addressed issues concerning segregation in public schools. The case originated in 1949, when parents from Anacostia, an area in Washington, DC, petitioned the Board of Education of the District of Columbia to allow all races to attend a new school. The request was denied. A lawsuit was brought before the District Court for the District of Columbia on behalf of a student named Bolling and other students to admit them to the all white school. The case was dismissed by the District Court and taken to the Supreme Court. The Supreme Court ruled that the school had to be desegregated based on the Fifth Amendment.

Civil Rights Act of 1964

The Civil Rights Act of 1964 was passed to protect the right of both black men and of women. It served as part of the foundation for the women's right movement. The act was a catalyst for change in the United States, as it made it illegal to engage in acts of discrimination in public facilities, in government, and in employment. The Civil Rights Act prohibited unequal voter registration, prohibited discrimination in all public facilities involved in interstate commerce, supported desegregating public schools, insured equal protection for blacks in federally funded programs, and banned employment discrimination.

Age Discrimination in Employment Act

The Age Discrimination in Employment Act of 1967 makes it illegal for employers to discriminate against people who are forty years old or greater in age. The act establishes standards for employer provided pensions and benefits and mandates that information regarding the needs of older workers be made publicly available. In addition to generally banning age discrimination, the ADEA specifies particular actions that are illegal. Employers may not specify that individuals of a certain age are preferred or are conversely restricted from applying to job ads. Age limits are only permitted to be mentioned in job ads if age has been shown to be a bona fide occupational qualification. The act stipulates that it is illegal to discriminate against age through apprenticeship programs, and that it is illegal to restrict benefits to older employees. However, employers are permitted to lower the benefits provided to older employees based on age if the expense of providing fewer or lesser benefits is equivalent to the expense of providing benefits to younger employees.

Loving vs. Virginia

Loving versus Virginia was a 1967 Supreme Court case. The decision that resulted from the case ruled that a particular law in Virginia known as the Racial Integrity Act of 1924 was unconstitutional. The Virginia law had prohibited interracial marriage, and therefore with the Supreme Court ruling put an end to race-based restrictions on marriage. The case originated when Mildred Jeter and Richard Loving, an interracial Virginia couple that was married in Washington, D.C. due to a Virginia state law prohibiting interracial marriage returned to Virginia and received charges of violating the interracial marriage ban. After pleading guilty, the couple was forced to move to D.C. to avoid a jail sentence, where they brought their case to the Supreme Court on the premise that their Fourteenth Amendment rights had been violated. The Supreme Court found that the Virginia law was unconstitutional and overturned the conviction that the couple had been charged with.

Civil Rights Act of 1968

The Civil Rights Act of 1968 was passed following the passing of the Civil Rights Act of 1964. The act made it illegal to discriminate against individuals during the sale, rental, or financing of housing. Therefore the act is also referred to as the Fair Housing Act of 1968. The act made it illegal to refuse to sell or rent housing based on race, color, religion, or national origin. It also made it illegal to advertise housing for sale or rent and to specify a preference to rent or sell the property to an individual of a particular race, color, religion, or national origin. In addition, the act ensured protection for civil rights workers.

Jones vs. Mayer

Jones versus Mayer was a 1968 Supreme Court case. In this case, the United States Supreme Court ruled that Congress has the authority to regulate the sale of private property for the purpose of preventing racial discrimination. This United States Supreme Court ruling was based on a legal statue that stipulates that it is illegal in the United States to commit acts of racial discrimination, both privately and publicly, when selling or renting property. The United States Supreme Court ruled that the Congressional power to uphold the statute extends from the power of Congress to uphold the Thirteenth Amendment.

Roe vs. Wade

Roe vs. Wade was a controversial 1973 U.S. Supreme Court case. The case originated in 1970 in Texas, which had an anti-abortion law. The plaintiff was an unmarried pregnant woman who was assigned the name "Jane Roe" to protect her identity. Texas anti-abortion law characterized the acts of having or attempting to perform an abortion as crimes, with the exception of cases in which an abortion could save the life of a mother. The lawsuit argued that the Texas law was unconstitutionally vague and was not consistent with the rights guaranteed by the First, Fourth, Fifth, Ninth, and Fourteenth Amendments. While the Texas court ruled in favor of Roe, it did not rule that Texas had to discontinue the enforcement of its anti-abortion law. Roe appealed to the Supreme Court in 1971, and the court's decision in 1973 struck down Texas's abortion laws. The case overturned most state laws prohibiting abortion.

The Pregnancy Discrimination Act

The Pregnancy Discrimination Act was passed in 1978 as an amendment to the sex discrimination clause of the Civil Rights Act of 1964. The Pregnancy Discrimination Act stipulated that people cannot be discriminated against due to pregnancy, childbirth, or medical issues related to pregnancy or childbirth. If a person becomes pregnant, gives birth, or has related medical conditions they must receive treatment that is equivalent to that received by other employees and also receive equal benefits as other employees. The Family and Medical Leave Act was passed in 1993 to advance protections under the Pregnancy Discrimination Act.

Regents of the University of California vs. Bakke

Regents of the University of California versus Bakke was a 1978 Supreme Court case that banned quota systems in the college admissions process but ruled that programs providing advantages to minorities are constitutionally sound. The case originated when Allan Bakke, a white male who was a strong student, applied to the University of California at Davis Medical School and was rejected. The school had a program that reserved admissions spots for minority applicants; the program had grown along with the overall size of the school since its opening in 1968. Bakke complained to the school but was still not admitted and he finally brought his case before the Superior Court of California. The California court ruled in favor of Bakke, who claimed that he had been discriminated against because of his race, and the school appealed to the U.S. Supreme Court. The Supreme Court ruled that race could be used as one factor by discriminatory boards such as college admissions boards; however quotas were ruled to be discriminatory.

The Americans with Disabilities Act

The Americans with Disabilities Act was passed in 1990 and signed by President George Bush. The act is a broad civil rights law banning discrimination against individuals with disabilities. The act offers protections against discrimination to Americans with disabilities that are similar to those offered by the Civil Rights Act of 1964. However, protections are not provided to individuals who have alcoholism or who identify themselves with transsexuality. There are a number of controversies surrounding the American with Disabilities Act. There are those who argue that the act has not really made many advances in terms of limiting discrimination against individuals with disabilities due to its nature as generally requiring a complaint to be filed before action is taken against disability discrimination.

Civil Rights Act of 1991

The Civil Rights Act of 1991 is a statute. It was passed as a result of a number of Supreme Court decisions that restricted the rights of individuals who had sued their employers on the basis of discrimination. The passing of the Civil Rights Act of 1991 was the first time since the Civil Rights Act of 1964 was passed that modifications were made to the rights granted under federal laws to individuals in cases involving employment discrimination. Specifically, the Civil Rights Act of 1991 granted the right to a trial by jury to individuals involved in cases of employment discrimination and it also addressed for the first time the potential for emotional distress damages and limited the amount awarded by a jury in such cases.

Planned Parenthood vs. Casey

Planned Parenthood of Southeastern Pennsylvania vs. Casey was a 1992 Supreme Court case that challenged the constitutionality of Pennsylvania abortion laws. The case was brought before the U.S. District Court for the Eastern District of Pennsylvania by abortion clinics and physicians to challenge four clauses of the Pennsylvania Abortion Control Act of 1982 as unconstitutional under Roe v.

Wade. The District Court ruled that all of the clauses of the Pennsylvania act were unconstitutional. The case was then appealed to the Third Circuit Court of Appeals, which ruled to uphold all of the clauses except for one requiring notification of a husband prior to abortion. The case was then appealed to the Supreme Court, which ruled to uphold constitutional right to have an abortion, thereby upholding Roe v. Wade.

Adarand Constructors, Inc. vs. Peña

Adarand Constructors, Inc. versus Peña was a 1995 United States Supreme Court case in which the court ruled that any racial classifications that are instituted by representatives of federal, state, or local governments have to be reviewed and analyzed by a court. The court that reviews such racial classifications must abide by a policy of strict scrutiny. Strict scrutiny represents the highest standard of Supreme Court review. Racial classifications are deemed constitutional solely under circumstances in which they are being used as specific measures to advance critical and important governmental interests. The ruling of the Supreme Court in this case requiring strict scrutiny as a standard of review for racial classifications overturned the case of Metro Broadcasting, Inc. v. FCC, in which the Supreme Court established a two-level method of reviewing and analyzing racial classifications.

Grutter vs. Bollinger

Grutter versus Bollinger was a 2003 Supreme Court case that upheld an affirmative action policy of the University of Michigan Law School admissions process. The case originated in 1996 when Barbara Grutter, a white in-state resident with a strong academic record applied to the law school and was denied admission. In 1997 she filed a lawsuit claiming that her rejection was based on racial discrimination and violated her Fourteenth Amendment rights, as well as Title VI of the Civil Rights Act of 1964. The case was heard in 2001 in a U.S. District Court, which ruled that the university's admissions policies were unconstitutional. In 2002 the case was appealed to the Sixth Circuit Court of Appeals, which overturned the lower court's decision. The case was then appealed to the U.S. Supreme Court in 2003, which ruled that the school's affirmative action policy could remain in place, upholding the case of Regents of the University of California v. Bakke permitting race to be a factor in admissions but banning quotas.

The Employment Non-Discrimination Act

The Employment Non-Discrimination Act is a proposed United States federal law that has not yet been passed. The Employment Non-Discrimination Act would ban employers from discriminating against their employees based on their sexual orientation. A number of states have already passed laws that ban discrimination based on sexual orientation, including California, Connecticut, the District of Columbia, Hawaii, Maryland, Massachusetts, Minnesota, Nevada, New Hampshire, New Jersey, New Mexico, New York, Rhode Island, Vermont, and Wisconsin. As it is currently proposed, the federal law would not protect transgender or intersexual individuals from discrimination.

The President

The President of the U.S. is the Head of the Executive Branch. The powers of the President are defined by the U.S. Constitution, and include the power to act as Commander in Chief of U.S. Armed Forces; as such, the President can authorize the use of troops without a declaration of war. To declare war, the President must receive approval from Congress. The President must also receive the consent of Congress when using the power to make treaties, appoint the heads of Executive Branch departments, and appoint ambassadors, Supreme Court judges, federal judges, and other officials. The President also has the power to receive foreign ambassadors and other representatives of foreign nations; to provide a yearly State of the Union Address; to recommend legislation; to convene and adjourn Congress; to ensure that laws are carried out; to fill administrative openings when Congress is in recess; and to issue reprieves and pardons for crimes against the United States.

The President of the United States is elected for a term of four years. The President may serve for a maximum of two terms. In order to be the President of the United States of America, an individual must be a natural born citizen of the United States. Candidates for the position of United States President must also be at least thirty-five years of age. Finally, in order to become President of the United States of America, an individual must have been a resident of the United States for at least fourteen years.

The President can recommend legislation to members of Congress, who can then introduce it as a bill. Only Congress can create legislation, but the President's approval of a bill is significant in determining whether it will pass. The President may sign a bill into law, veto a bill, or do nothing with it once it has passed Congress and been sent to the President for approval. If the President signs a bill into law, only the Supreme Court can then dismiss it by finding it unconstitutional. If a bill is vetoed, it is sent back to Congress without the President's signature, where Congress can override the veto with two-thirds approval. If the President does nothing with a bill, and Congress is in session ten business days following the receipt of the bill by the President, it becomes law without the President's signature; if Congress adjourns within ten business days, the bill dies, which is referred to as a pocket veto. The President can only veto a bill in its entirety.

Presidential Budget

The Budget and Accounting Act of 1921 requires the President to submit an annual document to Congress by the first Monday of February containing the proposed spending plan for the Federal Government in the upcoming fiscal year. The budget is essentially a set of goals with associated costs. The purpose of the budget is to provide a guide for Congress to use when determining how much money to spend, what to spend money on, and how to raise money to meet spending goals. The Office of Management and Budget helps the President with the annual spending plan. Federal appropriations must be approved by Congress. When Congress receives the spending plan, the House of Representatives establishes a level of spending for the Federal Government. Finally, Congress determines how this level of spending will be allocated for various Federal actions.

Presidential Impeachment

By definition, impeachment is actually the first step in the process of removing an official from office by a charge of crime or misconduct while in office. In the case of the President of the United States, if the House of Representatives believes that the President has committed criminal activity or engaged in misconduct while in office, specifically treason, bribery, and other high crimes and misdemeanors, by majority vote the House can impeach the President. After the House has impeached the President, the Senate examines the case and votes to convict the President or not. If two-thirds of the Senate votes to convict the President, he is removed from his position. The process of impeachment is overseen by the Chief Justice of the Supreme Court.

Presidential Succession Act of 1947

The Presidential Succession Act of 1947 specifies the order of succession if the President of the United States is unable to carry out the duties and responsibilities of the office of the President due to death, resignation, removal from office, or due to conditions that otherwise render the President incapacitated. In such a situation, the office of the President will be filled by the following people, in order: Vice President, Speaker of the House, President Pro Tempore of the Senate, Secretary of State, Secretary of the Treasury, Secretary of Defense, Attorney General, Secretary of the Interior, Secretary of Agriculture, Secretary of Commerce, Secretary of Labor, Secretary of Health and Human Services, Secretary of Housing and Urban Development, Secretary of Transportation, Secretary of Energy, Secretary of Education, Secretary of Veterans Affairs, and finally Secretary of Homeland Security.

President's Cabinet

The President's Cabinet is comprised of the heads of the executive departments, who advise the President on issues related to their respective departments on a weekly basis. Members of the Cabinet include the Vice President, the Attorney General, and the Secretaries of Agriculture, Commerce, Defense, Education, Energy, Health and Human

Services, Homeland Security, Housing and Urban Development, Interior, Labor, State, Transportation, Treasury, and Veterans Affairs. Department heads are appointed by the President and confirmed by a majority vote in the Senate. They remain in their positions for the length of the President's administration, and when a new administration begins, the heads of the executive departments are expected to leave their positions. The President can fire the head of an executive department without approval from Congress.

The Secretary of State

The Secretary of State is a member of the President's Cabinet and is the head of the Department of State, which was established in 1789. The Department of State is responsible for advising the President on foreign policy, implementing foreign policy, and working on behalf of American interests internationally. The Department of State works with citizens of the United States, Congress, other departments and agencies within United States government, and foreign governments. The Department of State is responsible for negotiating international treaties and agreements and representing the United States in international organizations, including the United Nations, and at international meetings.

The Secretary of Defense

The Secretary of Defense is a member of the President's Cabinet and is the head of the Department of Defense, which was established in 1947. The Department of Defense is responsible for protecting United States security by supplying armed forces. The armed forces of the United States are comprised of the Army, Navy, Marine Corps, and Air Force. The Reserve and National Guard also exist as part of the Department of Defense to assist in case of emergency. The Defense Department is also staffed by civilian employees. The Secretary of Defense is responsible for directing and overseeing the Department of Defense.

The Secretary of the Treasury

The Secretary of the Treasury is a member of the President's Cabinet and is the head of the Department of the Treasury, which was established in 1789. The Department of the Treasury is responsible for developing and recommending economic, financial, tax, and fiscal policies, acting as the U.S. government's primary financial agent, enforcing laws, and producing coins and currency. The Secretary of the Treasury is the President's key advisor on national and international financial, economic, and tax policy. The Secretary of the Treasury also assists with developing wide-ranging economic policies and handles public debt.

The Secretary of the Interior

The Secretary of the interior is a member of the President's Cabinet and is the head of the Department of the Interior, which was established in 1849. The Department of the Interior is responsible for protecting and ensuring access to the natural and cultural resources of the United States. The Department of the Interior is also responsible for ensuring that the United States upholds its responsibilities to Native American tribes. The Department of the Interior administers the public lands and minerals, national parks, national wildlife refuges, and western water resources of the United States. The employees of the Department of the Interior work on issues related to migratory wildlife conservation, historic preservation, endangered species, the protection and restoration of lands that have undergone surface mining, mapping, and geological, hydrological, and biological sciences.

The Attorney General

The Attorney General is a member of the President's Cabinet and is the head of the Department of Justice, which was established in 1870. The Department of Justice is responsible for providing legal counsel for the people of the United States. The Department of Justice consists of lawyers, investigators, and federal agents. The Attorney General is responsible for directing the Department of Justice, and in rare circumstances will represent the United States government in Supreme Court cases. The Attorney General also advises the President and the other heads of the executive departments on legal matters.

The Secretary of Commerce

The Secretary of Commerce is a member of the President's Cabinet and is the head of the Department of Commerce, which was established in 1903. The Department of Commerce is responsible for furthering international trade, economic growth, and technological advancement opportunities for the United States. The Department of Commerce works to increase the competitiveness of the United States in the international economy and decrease unfair competition in international trade. The Department of Commerce also conducts social and economic statistical analysis, conducts science, engineering and technology research, and makes efforts to advance knowledge and utilization of the physical environment and ocean resources. In addition, the Department of Commerce issues patents and trademarks. The Department of Commerce also researches and makes policies related to telecommunications, aids in fostering domestic economic growth, and works to further the development of minority owned businesses.

The Secretary of Commerce advises the President on issues pertaining to the industrial and commercial areas of the United States economy.

The Secretary of Agriculture

The Secretary of Agriculture is a member of the President's Cabinet and is the head of the Department of Agriculture, which was established in 1862. The Department of Agriculture is responsible for efforts to maintain and increase agricultural profits, as well as efforts to foster international markets for United States agricultural products. One of the purposes of the Department of Agriculture is to aid in alleviating poverty, hunger, and malnutrition. Another goal of the Department of Agriculture is to improve agricultural production by aiding in the protection of natural resources. The Department of Agriculture is responsible for ensuring the quality and safety of food by the use of inspection and grading activities.

The Secretary of Health and Human Services

The Secretary of Health and Human Services is a member of the President's Cabinet and is the head of the Department of Health and Human Services, which was established in 1953. The Department of Health and Human Services is responsible for protecting the health of the citizens of the United States and providing vital human services. The Department of Health and Human Services conducts health and social science research, conducts research aimed at preventing disease, researches and provides immunization services, works to ensure food and drug safety, manages Medicare and Medicaid, provides health information technology, provides financial aid and services for low-income families, works to better maternal and infant health, manages the program Head Start for pre-school students, supports community programs, works to reduce child abuse and domestic violence, supports substance abuse treatment and prevention, supports services for the elderly, ensures health services for Native Americans, and prepares for medical emergencies. The Secretary of Health and Human Services provides advice to the President on issues regarding health, welfare, and income security.

The Secretary of Labor

The Secretary of Labor is a member of the President's Cabinet and is the head of the Department of Labor, which was established in 1913. The Department of Labor is responsible for advancing the well-being of workers in the United States, bettering working conditions, and increasing the employment opportunities available to workers. To meet these responsibilities, the Department of Labor administers Federal labor laws to ensure the rights of employees to a safe working environment, a minimum wage, overtime pay, unemployment insurance, and workers' compensation. The Department of Labor also administers labor laws to ensure that discrimination does not occur in the workplace. Other efforts that the Department of Labor makes in the interest of workers involve the protection of employee pension rights, job training programs, job placement programs, improving collective bargaining ability, and monitoring economic indicators related to employment.

The Secretary of Transportation

The Secretary of Transportation is a member of the President's Cabinet and is the head of the Department of Transportation, which was established in

1966. The Department of Transportation is responsible for developing transportation policy in the United States, including with relation to highway planning, development, and construction, mass transportation in urban areas, railroads, aviation, and the safety and security of the waterways, ports, highways, and oil and gas pipelines of the United States. The Department of Transportation develops transportation policy in coordination with state and local agencies and organizations. Transportation policies greatly impact other sectors, including land management, resource conservation, and technology.

The Secretary of Housing and Urban Development

The Secretary of Housing and Urban Development is a member of the President's Cabinet and is the head of the Department of Housing and Urban Development, which was established in 1965. The Department of Housing and Urban Development is responsible for developing programs and policies related to housing and community development in the United States. Specifically, the Department of Housing and Urban Development administers housing assistance programs, fosters State and local involvement in addressing housing and community development issues, and promotes donations from private house building and mortgage lending companies to housing and community development programs.

The Secretary of Education

The Secretary of Education is a member of the President's Cabinet and is the head of the Department of Education, which was established in 1979. The Department of Education is responsible for developing policies and administering federal assistance for educational programs. The goal of the Department of Education is to provide equal access to education for all citizens of the United States and to foster quality educational programs. The Secretary of Education provides advice to the President related to education policies and programs.

The Secretary of Energy

The Secretary of Energy is a member of the President's Cabinet and is the head of the Department of Energy, which was established in 1977. The Department of Energy is responsible for developing and sharing technical, scientific and educational information with leaders and policy-makers in order to foster efficient energy consumption, the development and implementation of a wide variety of energy sources, economic production and competition, higher standards of environmental quality, and a secure and stable defense program for the United States.

The Secretary of Homeland Security

The Secretary of Homeland Security is a member of the President's Cabinet and is the head of the Department of Homeland Security, which was established in 2003. The Department of Homeland Security is responsible for efforts aimed at preventing terrorist attacks against the United States. The Department of Homeland Security is also responsible for efforts to reduce the susceptibility of the United States to terrorism. In addition, the Department of Homeland Security is responsible for efforts aimed at reducing the devastation and suffering from potential terrorist attacks and natural disasters.

The Secretary of Veterans Affairs

The Secretary of Veterans Affairs is a member of the President's Cabinet and is the head of the Department of Veterans Affairs, which was established in 1988. The Department of Veterans Affairs is responsible for administering programs with the goal of providing benefits to veterans and their families. Specifically, the Department of Veterans Affairs provides funds for disabilities or death that result from military service, pensions, educational benefits, rehabilitation benefits, home loan guaranties, burial benefits, and a healthcare program that encompasses nursing homes, clinics, and medical centers for veterans. The Department of Veterans Affairs is made up of the Veterans Health Administration, the Veterans Benefits Administration, and the National Cemetery Administration, each of which has a central office and field offices.

Legislative Branch

The Legislative branch was established by Article I of the United States Constitution. The Legislative branch is responsible for making laws. In the United States the Legislative branch is a bicameral system, which means that it is divided into two houses, the House of Representatives and the Senate. The bicameral system ensures that checks and balances exist within the Legislative branch. Representatives and Senators are elected by the people in the state that they represent. Also included in the Legislative branch are all of the agencies that provide support to Congress, including the Government Printing Office, the Library of Congress, the Congressional Budget Office, the General Accounting Office, and the Architect of the Capitol.

The Congress

The Congress represents one part of the legislative branch in the United States. Congress is composed of two chambers known as the House of Representatives and the Senate. The two chamber system is referred to as a bicameral legislative system. Congress is responsible for writing, debating, and passing bills. Once bills are passed by Congress, they go to the President of the United States to be reviewed, approved and signed into law. Congress is also responsible for investigating issues that are important on a national level and for overseeing both the executive and judicial branches. Elections are held every two years for all 435 members of the House of Representatives and for one third of the members of the Senate. Congress begins a new session every January after Congressional elections. Congress convenes once a year, typically from January 3rd through July 31st.

Article I Section 8 of the Constitution gives Congress the power to establish and collect taxes; to pay debts; to provide for the defense of the country; to borrow money on credit; to regulate domestic and international commerce; to establish immigration policy; to establish bankruptcies laws; to create money; to establish a postal system; to protect patents and intellectual property rights; to create lower courts; to control and protect citizens and ships in international waters; to declare war; to establish and maintain an army and a navy; to maintain National Guard readiness; and to exercise control over the District of Columbia and other federal property. Section 8 also includes a clause known as the Elastic Clause which gives Congress the power to pass any law necessary for carrying out the actions over which it has power.

Oversight Powers of Congress

Congress is afforded certain oversight powers that enable it to exert influence over the Executive branch of the U.S. government. Congressional oversight is significant for a number of reasons; it stops waste and fraud; upholds civil liberties and rights; makes sure that the executive branch is in compliance with the law; serves as a means of gathering data and information that is necessary to make laws and to inform the public; and provides a means for evaluating the performance of the executive branch of government. Congressional oversight is applicable to the Cabinet, to all executive agencies, to regulatory commissions, and to the President.

There are a number of ways that Congress can exercise oversight of the executive branch of government in order to ensure a system of checks and balances and to exert influence over public policy. Some of the mechanisms available to Congress include the use of committee hearings, discussions and meetings with the President and other executive officials, reports from the President, the power of the Senate to advise and approve nominations made and treaties drafted by the president and to hold trials for impeached officials, the power of the House to impeach, the ability of Congress to address the order of succession of the Presidency, membership in government commissions, and studies by Congressional committees and Congressional support agencies.

The Committee System

The Congressional committee system started in 1789. Congressional committees are created to address political, social, and economic changes. Both the House and the Senate have their own committees, and there are also joint committees between both houses. To address an increasing number of issues that must be discussed, subcommittees have also formed. Committees are responsible for investigating each bill that is proposed to Congress. This investigation could include holding hearings where expert witnesses provide information and facts that are relevant to the bill. Once the committee has heard all the facts, it either recommends the bill as it was originally written or it suggests that the bill should be passed with amendments. Occasionally bills are tabled, or put aside, which stops consideration of those bills. Once a bill is passed in each house, a committee called the conference committee works to find common ground between House and Senate versions of the bill. After both houses agree to the same version of the bill and it passes a final vote, it is sent to the President.

The House of Representatives

Members of the House of Representatives are elected for two year terms. Each state has at least one Representative, and the number of Representatives in each state depends upon its population as reported in the most recent census. Each state is divided into congressional districts. There is a Representative for every congressional district, who is elected by the voters in that district. There are 435 members of the House of Representatives, and Congress has the power to alter the total membership. A Representative must be at least 25 years old, a citizen of the United States for at least seven years, and a resident of the state to which they are elected. The House of Representatives has the power of impeachment.

There are 435 members of the House of Representatives. Every member represents a region within a state; these regions are referred to as congressional districts and are based on population size. Congressional districts are established every ten years through the process of a population census which is carried out by the U.S. Census Bureau. The number of congressional districts in a state determines how many Representatives are from that state. Every state has at least one seat in the House. Representatives come not only from the fifty states but in addition five members represent Puerto Rico, Guam, American Samoa, the Virgin Islands, and D.C. These five members are not permitted to vote in Congress, but are permitted to engage in debates. The House is solely responsible for initiating laws that require citizens to pay taxes and for determining whether government officials should be tried for committing crimes against the U.S.

Standing Committees of the House of Representatives

Although Congressional committees are created to address changing political, social, and economic conditions, there are a number of committees that are permanent, or standing committees. The Standing Committees within the House of Representatives include the Agriculture Committee, the Appropriations Committee, the Armed Services Committee, the Banking and Financial Services Committee, the Budget Committee, the Commerce Committee, the Education and the Workforce Committee, the Government Reform and Oversight Committee, the House Administration Committee, the International Relations Committee, the Judiciary Committee, the Resources Committee, the Rules Committee, the Science Committee, the Small Business Committee, the Standards of Official Conduct Committee, the Transportation and Infrastructure Committee, the

Veterans' Affairs Committee, and the Ways and Means Committee.

Appropriations Committee
The House Committee on Appropriations was created in 1865. The committee has jurisdiction over the appropriation of money to government departments, the withdrawal of appropriations, and the transfer of unspent funds. The committee holds hearings to review budget recommendations and policies of the President and to review the financial factors used to come up with the budget. Subcommittees of the House Committee on Appropriations include the Subcommittee on Agriculture, Rural Development, Food and Drug Administration, and Related Agencies, the Subcommittee on Defense, the Subcommittee on Energy and Water Development, and Related Agencies, the Subcommittee on Foreign Operations, Export Financing and Related Programs, the Subcommittee on Homeland Security, the Subcommittee on Interior, Environment, and Related Agencies, the Subcommittee on Labor, Health and Human Services, Education, and Related Agencies, the Subcommittee on Military Quality of Life and Veterans Affairs, and Related Agencies, the Subcommittee on Science, the Departments of State, Justice, and Commerce, and Related Agencies, and the Subcommittee on Transportation, Treasury, and Housing and Urban Development, The Judiciary, District of Columbia.

Agriculture Committee
The House Committee on Agriculture was established in 1820. The committee has jurisdiction over the degradation of seeds, over the control of insect pests, and over the protection of fauna in forest reserves. The committee also has jurisdiction over agriculture, agricultural and industrial chemistry, agricultural colleges and laboratories, agricultural economics,

agricultural education extension services, agricultural production and marketing, prices of agricultural products and commodities, animal industries, animal disease, commodity exchanges, crop insurance, soil conservation, the dairy industry, entomology, plant quarantine, extension of farm credit and farm security, inspection of meat and seafood products, forestry, human nutrition and home economics, plant industry, soils, and agricultural engineering, rural electrification, rural development, and water conservation. Subcommittees include the Subcommittee on Conservation, Credit, Rural Development and Research, the Subcommittee on General Farm Commodities and Risk Management, the Subcommittee on Specialty Crops and Foreign Agriculture Programs, the Subcommittee on Department Operations, Oversight, Dairy, Nutrition and Forestry, and the Subcommittee on Livestock and Horticulture.

Budget Committee
The House Committee on the Budget is responsible for developing a budget resolution that establishes spending and revenue levels for federal programs. The committee has oversight over the laws and regulations that are relevant to the budget process, as well as over the agencies that hold the responsibility for the administration of such laws. Specifically, the committee has jurisdiction over the Budget and Accounting Act of 1920, the Congressional Budget Act of 1974, and the Emergency Balanced Budget and Deficit Control Act of 1985, and the agencies over which it holds jurisdiction include the Office of Management and Budget and the Congressional Budget Office. The committee also investigates tax expenditures and the impact of legislation on budget expenditures. In addition, the committee has jurisdiction over budget

priorities, budget enforcement, budget process reform, and direct spending and tax incentives.

Armed Services Committee
The House Committee on Armed Services has jurisdiction over matters related to defense and the Department of Defense, including the Departments of the Army, Navy and Air Force, ammunition storage facilities, forts, arsenals, and Army, Navy, and Air Force locations. In addition the committee has jurisdiction over the conservation, cultivation and use of naval oil reserves, as well as canals connecting oceans, the Merchant Marine Academy, and state Merchant Marine Academies. The committee also has jurisdiction over nuclear energy as it is applied within the military, tactical intelligence, matters related to the merchant marine which affect national security, the salaries and benefits of individuals who are in the armed forces, scientific R&D for the armed forces, the selective service, the size and makeup of the armed forces, soldiers and sailors homes, and materials required to provide defense. Subcommittees include the Tactical Air and Land Forces Subcommittee, the Readiness Subcommittee, the Terrorism, Unconventional Threats and Capabilities Subcommittee, the Military Personnel Subcommittee, the Strategic Forces Subcommittee, and the Projection Forces Subcommittee.

Education and the Workforce: Workforce Committee
The House Committee on Education and the Workforce was created in 1997. The committee has jurisdiction over issues concerning education and labor. The committee promotes efforts to improve health care, job training, and retirement security for workers. The committee also promotes efforts to advance opportunities for people, especially in the area of emerging knowledge. Specific

items on the agenda of the committee with regard to workforce include pension and retirement security for workers, access to health care and other benefits for workers, job training, adult education, and workforce development, welfare reform, protecting democratic rights for union members, health and safety, offering more scheduling and work arrangement choices and flexibility for workers, equal employment opportunity, civil rights, wages and hours of labor, workers' compensation, family and medical leave, the relationships between employers and employees.

Education and the Workforce: Education Committee

The House Committee on Education and the Workforce was created in 1997. The committee has jurisdiction over issues concerning education and labor. All levels of education are addressed by the committee, including elementary and secondary education programs, the No Child Left Behind Act, school choice for low-income individuals, special education, educator quality and educator training, scientific reading instruction, vocational and technical education, higher education programs, college access for low and middle-income individuals, financial aid, early childhood and preschool programs, Head Start, school lunch and nutrition, financial oversight of the U.S. Department of Education, care and treatment of at-risk children, child abuse prevention, child adoption, educational research and advancement, adult education, and anti-poverty programs.

Financial Services Committee

The House Committee on Financial Services has jurisdiction over banks and banking, stabilization of the economy, defense production, commodity, rent, and service prices, financial assistance for commerce and industry, insurance,

international finance, international financial and monetary organizations, money and credit, public and private housing, securities and exchanges, and urban development. The House Committee on Financial Services has several subcommittees, including the Subcommittee on Capital Markets, Insurance and Government Sponsored Enterprises, the Subcommittee on Domestic and International Monetary Policy, Trade and Technology, the Subcommittee on Financial Institutions and Consumer Credit, the Subcommittee on Housing and Community Opportunity, and the Subcommittee on Oversight and Investigations.

Energy and Commerce Committee

The House Committee on Energy and Commerce is the longest-standing committee in the House of Representatives. The committee has broad jurisdiction, including jurisdiction over issues pertaining to telecommunications, consumer protection, food and drug safety, public health, air quality, environmental health, supply and delivery of energy, and interstate and foreign commerce. The committee has jurisdiction over the Department of Energy, the Department of Health and Human Services, the Department of Transportation, the Federal Trade Commission, the Food and Drug Administration, and the Federal Communications Commission. Subcommittees of the House Committee on Energy and Commerce include the Subcommittee on Commerce, Trade and Consumer Protection, the Subcommittee on Energy and Air Quality, the Subcommittee on Environment and Hazardous Materials, the Subcommittee on Health, the Subcommittee on Oversight and Investigations, and the Subcommittee on Telecommunications and the Internet.

m ,mjurisdiction over a wide spectrum of issues and factors pertaining to the prevention of terrorist attacks on the U.S. particularly involving weapons that are characterized as nuclear and biological weapons. The subcommittees of the Committee on Homeland Security include the Subcommittee on Prevention of Nuclear and Biological Attack, the Subcommittee on Intelligence, Information Sharing, and Terrorism Risk Assessment, the Subcommittee on Economic Security, Infrastructure Protection, and Cybersecurity, the Subcommittee on Management, Integration, and Oversight, the Subcommittee on Emergency Preparedness, Science, and Technology, and the Subcommittee on Investigations.

Government Reform Committee
The Committee on Government Reform Committee is the most important legislative investigative and oversight committee. The committee has oversight over the National Guard, the Reserves, Homeland Security, the U.S. Postal Service, management reform, diploma mills, electronic voting, regulatory affairs, the Bureau of Economic Analysis, the Unfunded Mandates Reform Act, new dietary guidelines, the thrift savings plan, security clearance reform, federal agency contracting, the General Services Administration, information technology and information policy, intellectual property piracy, the Department of the interior's tribal recognition process, D.C., flu vaccine supply and state and local health preparedness, FDA post-marketing surveillance, USDA cattle surveillance, and twenty-first century healthcare. There are numerous subcommittees of the House Committee on Government Reform, including the Subcommittee on Criminal Justice, Drug Policy and Human Resources, the Subcommittee on Energy and Resources, the Subcommittee on Federalism and the Census, the

Subcommittee on Federal Workforce and Agency Organization, the Subcommittee on Government Management, Finance, and Accountability, the Subcommittee on National Security, Emerging Threats and International Relations, and the Subcommittee on Regulatory Affairs.

International Relations Committee
The House Committee on International Relations has jurisdiction over issues pertaining to international relations between the U.S. and other countries, procurement of property for U.S. embassies, the delineation of boundaries between the U.S. and other countries, export controls, nonproliferation of nuclear technology, foreign loans, international commodity agreements, international conferences and congresses, international education, international intervention and war, diplomacy, efforts to promote U.S. commercial interests globally, international economic policy, neutrality, protection of U.S. citizens abroad, the American Red Cross, trading with enemies, and the United Nations. Subcommittees of the House Committee on International Relations include the Subcommittee on Asia and the Pacific, the Subcommittee on Africa, Global Human Rights and International Operations, the Subcommittee on the Western Hemisphere, the Subcommittee on Europe and Emerging Threats, the Subcommittee on the Middle East and Central Asia, the Subcommittee on Oversight and Investigations, and the Subcommittee on International Terrorism and Nonproliferation.

Administration Committee
The Committee on House Administration is responsible for overseeing federal elections as well as the daily functions of the House of Representatives. Specifically, the Committee on House Administration has jurisdiction over the Library of Congress, statues and pictures,

the acceptance of or purchase of works of art for the Capitol, and the Botanic Garden. The Committee on House Administration also has jurisdiction over the purchase of books and manuscripts and the Smithsonian Institution. The Committee on House Administration is also responsible for the oversight of the establishment of other institutions similar to the Smithsonian Institution.

Resources Committee

The House Committee on Resources has jurisdiction over issues pertaining to fisheries and wildlife, forest reserves and national parks, forfeiture of land grants and alien ownership, the Geological Survey, international fishing agreements, interstate compacts related to allocation of water for irrigation, irrigation and reclamation, Native Americans, insular possessions of the U.S., military parks, battlefields, national cemeteries, the establishment of monuments and memorials, mineral land laws and claims, mineral resources on public land, mining interests, mining schools and laboratories, marine affairs, oceanography, petroleum conservation on public lands, preservation of prehistoric ruins, public lands, U.S. government relations with Native Americans and Native American tribes, and the trans-Alaska oil pipeline. Subcommittees include the Subcommittee on Energy and Mineral Resources, the Subcommittee on Fisheries and Oceans, the Subcommittee on Forests and Forest Health, the Subcommittee on National Parks, and the Subcommittee on Water and Power.

Judiciary Committee

The House Committee on the Judiciary was created in 1813. The committee has jurisdiction over the judiciary, both civil and criminal judicial proceedings, administrative practices and procedures, the apportionment of Representatives,

bankruptcy, mutiny, espionage, and counterfeiting, civil liberties, constitutional amendments, criminal law enforcement, federal courts and judges, local courts in U.S. territories and possessions, immigration policy, interstate compacts, cases against the U.S. government, members of Congress, national jails, patents, the Patent and Trademark Office, copyrights, trademarks, succession to the office of President, protection of trade and commerce against illegal obstacles and monopolies, revision and codification of statutes, the boundaries of states and territories, and activities that are considered treacherous and threatening to the security of the U.S. Subcommittees include the Subcommittee on Courts, the Internet, and Intellectual Property, the Subcommittee on Immigration, Border Security, and Claims, the Subcommittee on Commercial and Administrative Law, the Subcommittee on Crime, Terrorism, and Homeland Security, and the Subcommittee on the Constitution.

Science Committee

The House Committee on Science has jurisdiction over issues pertaining to all federal scientific research and development that is not military related. The committee has jurisdiction over the National Aeronautics and Space Administration, the Department of Energy, the Environmental Protection Agency, the National Science Foundation, the Federal Aviation Administration, the National Oceanic and Atmospheric Administration, the National Institute of Standards and Technology, the Federal Emergency Management Agency, the U.S. Fire Administration, and the U.S. Geological Survey. Subcommittees of the House Committee on Science include the Subcommittee on Environment, Technology, and Standards, the Subcommittee on Energy, the

Subcommittee on Research, and the Subcommittee on Space and Aeronautics.

Rules Committee

The House Committee on Rules has two subcommittees. The first subcommittee is the Subcommittee on the Rules and Organization of the House. This subcommittee has responsibilities concerning issues regarding the relationship between the House of Representatives and the Senate, as well as issues regarding the relationship between Congress and the Judicial Branch. The Subcommittee on the Rules and Organization of the House also has responsibilities related to the internal operations of the House of Representatives. The second subcommittee is the Subcommittee on the Legislative and Budget Process. This subcommittee has responsibilities concerning issues regarding the relationship between Congress and the Executive Branch. The Subcommittee on the Legislative and Budget Process also has responsibilities related to the Congressional budget process.

Standards of Official Conduct Committee

The House Committee on Standards of Official Conduct implements the ethics program for the House of Representatives, as each branch of the federal government has the responsibility of implementing its own ethics program. Each house of the legislative branch has its own ethics committee to implement its ethics program; the counterpart to the House Committee on Standards of Official Conduct is the Senate Select Committee on Ethics. The House Committee on Standards of Official Conduct has jurisdiction over issues pertaining to the House Code of Official Conduct. The committee has jurisdiction to create or administer standards of official conduct, to investigate violations of the code of official conduct, laws and regulations, to

provide reports to government authorities of evidence of violations of laws, to give opinions about the appropriateness of the conduct of individuals associated with the House of Representatives, and to review requests for exceptions to the gift rule, and over the Ethics in Government Act and the Foreign Gifts the Decorations Act.

Small Business Committee

The House Committee on Small Business has jurisdiction over issues pertaining to the Small Business Administration, financial and management programs and technical assistance programs for small business, advocacy for small business, issues related to veterans and small businesses, technology and research assistance programs for small businesses, the Small Business Technology Transfer program, federal procurement, government competition and regulatory flexibility, paperwork reduction, government regulation, taxation, energy, the Government Performance and Results Act, empowerment for small businesses in high risk areas, workforce issues, health care, pensions, e-commerce, telecommunications, international trade, self employment, manufacturing, agricultural and rural matters, and review of relevant regulations. The subcommittees of the House Committee on Small Business include the Subcommittee on Workforce, Empowerment, and Government Programs, the Subcommittee on Regulatory Reform and Oversight, the Subcommittee on Tax, Finance, and Exports, and the Subcommittee on Rural Enterprises, Agriculture, and Technology.

Veterans' Affairs Committee

The House Committee on Veterans' Affairs has jurisdiction over issues pertaining to veterans in a broad sense. The committee also has jurisdiction over pensions for veterans of all wars, and over life insurance provided by the federal government for veterans of the armed services. In addition, the House Committee on Veterans' Affairs has jurisdiction over issues pertaining to the compensation of veterans and over vocational training and educational programs for veterans. The committee also has jurisdiction over veterans hospitals, medical services for veterans, civil relief for sailors and soldiers, over services that assist individuals who have served in the armed forces in acclimating from life in the armed forces back into civilian life, and over national cemeteries. The committee has specific jurisdiction over the Department of Veterans Affairs. Subcommittees include the Subcommittee on Disability Assistance and Memorial Affairs, the Subcommittee on Economic Opportunity, the Subcommittee on Health, and the Subcommittee on Oversight and Investigations.

Transportation and Infrastructure Committee
The House Committee on Transportation and Infrastructure has jurisdiction over issues pertaining to aviation, the Coast Guard and maritime transportation, economic development, public buildings, emergency management, highways, public transit, pipelines, railways, and water resources and environmental issues. The subcommittees of the House Committee on Transportation and Infrastructure include the Subcommittee on Aviation, the Subcommittee on the Coast Guard and Maritime Transportation, the Subcommittee on Economic Development, Public Buildings and Emergency Management, the Subcommittee on Highways, Transit and Pipelines, the Subcommittee on Railroads, and the Subcommittee on Water Resources and Environment.

House Permanent Select Committee on Intelligence
The House Permanent Select Committee on Intelligence has the responsibility for overseeing many government organizations and their activities, including the Central Intelligence Agency, the Defense Intelligence Agency, the Department of Defense, the Department of Energy, the Department of Homeland Security, the Department of Justice, the Department of State, the Department of Treasury, the Federal Bureau of Investigation, the National Geospatial-Intelligence Agency, the National Reconnaissance Office, the National Security Agency, the Office of Naval Intelligence, the U.S. Air Force Intelligence, Surveillance, and Reconnaissance, the U.S. Army Intelligence and Security Command, the U.S. Coast Guard, and the U.S. Marine Corps Intelligence Department. Subcommittees of the House Permanent Select Committee on Intelligence include the Subcommittee on Terrorism/HUMINT, Analysis and Counterintelligence, the Subcommittee on Technical and Tactical Intelligence, the Subcommittee on Intelligence Policy, and the Subcommittee on Oversight.

Ways and Means Committee
The House Committee on Ways and Means has jurisdiction over customs, collection districts, ports, reciprocal trade agreements, broad efforts to generate revenue, efforts to generate revenue that are specifically associated with U.S. insular possessions, U.S. government debt, deposit of public funds, duties on goods, organizations that are exempt from paying taxes, and social security. Subcommittees of the House Committee on Ways and Means include the Subcommittee on Trade, the Subcommittee on Oversight, the Subcommittee on Health, the Subcommittee on Social Security, the

Subcommittee on Human Resources, and the Subcommittee on Select Revenue Measures.

The Senate

Senators are elected for terms of six years. The Senate is composed of two Senators from each state. Every two years one third of the Senate is up for re-election. Senators were originally chosen by their state legislatures, but with the passing of the 17th Amendment in 1913 Senators are now elected directly by voters within their state. A Senator must be at least 30 years old, a citizen of the United States for at least nine years, and a resident of the state to which they are elected. The Senate has the power to try all impeachments.

There are 100 members of the United States Senate. The U.S. Constitution stipulates that the Vice President of the United States controls the Senate and is therefore referred to as the president of the Senate. However, in reality the Vice President is not regularly in attendance when the Senate is in session; rather, the Vice President is typically only in attendance during significant ceremonial events and when he is required to vote to break a tie within the Senate. The Senate is solely responsible for either confirming or disapproving of treaties that are drafted by the United States President. The Senate is also solely responsible for either confirming or disapproving of appointments made by the United States President, including Cabinet-level appointments, officers, Supreme Court judges, and ambassadors. In addition, the Senate is solely responsible for trying government officials who commit crimes against the United States.

Standing Committees of the House of Representatives

Although Congressional committees are created to address changing political, social, and economic conditions, there are a number of committees that are permanent, or standing committees. The Standing Committees within the House of Representatives include the Agriculture Committee, the Appropriations Committee, the Armed Services Committee, the Banking and Financial Services Committee, the Budget Committee, the Commerce Committee, the Education and the Workforce Committee, the Government Reform and Oversight Committee, the House Administration Committee, the International Relations Committee, the Judiciary Committee, the Resources Committee, the Rules Committee, the Science Committee, the Small Business Committee, the Standards of Official Conduct Committee, the Transportation and Infrastructure Committee, the Veterans' Affairs Committee, and the Ways and Means Committee.

Standing Committees of the Senate

Although Congressional committees are created to address changing political, social, and economic conditions, there are a number of committees that are permanent or standing committees. The Standing Committees within the Senate include the Agriculture, Nutrition, and Forestry Committee, the Appropriations Committee, the Armed Services Committee, the Banking Committee, the Budget Committee, the Commerce, Science, and Transportation Committee, the Energy and Natural Resources Committee, the Environment and Public Works Committee, the Finance Committee, the Foreign Relations Committee, the Governmental Affairs Committee, the Health, Education, Labor, and Pension Committee, the Indian Affairs Committee, the Judiciary Committee, the Rules and Administration Committee, the Small Business Committee, and the Veterans' Affairs Committee.

Agriculture, Nutrition, and Forestry Committee

The Standing Committee on Agriculture, Nutrition, and Forestry was created in the year 1825. The committee writes legislation that addresses nutrition and food programs, the promotion of United States agricultural products in global markets, the development of rural areas, agricultural research, and conservation programs. The main legislation associated with the committee is known as the Farm Bill. Subcommittees of the Senate Standing Committee on Agriculture, Nutrition, and Forestry include the Subcommittee on Production and Price Competitiveness, the Subcommittee on Forestry, Conservation, and Rural Revitalization, the Subcommittee on Research, Nutrition, and General Legislation.

Appropriations Committee

The Senate Standing Committee on Appropriations was created in 1867. The committee is the biggest in the U.S. Senate. It is responsible for appropriating funds before money from the U.S. treasury can be spent. The committee allocates money to government agencies, departments, and organizations every year. Appropriations may not exceed the budget limits established by the Senate Budget Committee. There are twelve subcommittees of the Appropriations Committee that review the President's budget requests, listen to expert testimonies, and draft spending plans. Subcommittees pass information they gather to the Senate Appropriations Committee, which can review and change spending bills before passing them to the Senate to be considered. Subcommittees

include Agriculture, Rural Development, and Related Agencies; Commerce, Justice, and Science; Defense; District of Columbia; Energy and Water, Homeland Security; Interior and Related Agencies; Labor, Health and Human Services, Education and Related Agencies; Legislative Branch; Military Construction and Veterans Affairs; State, Foreign Operations, and Related Programs; Transportation, Treasury the Judiciary, Housing and Urban Development, and Related Agencies.

Banking, Housing, and Urban Affairs Committee

The Senate Standing Committee on Banking, Housing, and Urban Affairs is concerned with financial institutions, price control for commodities, rents and services, deposit insurance, maintaining a stable economy and keeping up defense production, promoting exports and stimulating foreign trade, establishing export controls, federal monetary policy, financial assistance for commerce and industry, issuing and redeeming notes, money and credit, the building of nursing homes, public and private housing, renegotiation of Government contracts, urban development and public transportation. Beneath the full committee are the Subcommittee on Securities and Investment, the Subcommittee on Financial Institutions, the Subcommittee on Housing and Transportation, the Subcommittee on Economic Policy, and the Subcommittee on International Trade and Finance.

Armed Services Committee

The Senate Standing Committee on Armed Services is concerned with aeronautical and space matters associated with military operations and weapons development; defense; the Department of Defense, the Department of the Army, the Department of the Navy, and the Department of the Air Force; the

Panama Canal; research and development associated with and carried out by the military; nuclear energy issues that are related to national security; naval petroleum reserves outside of Alaska; salaries and benefits for military personnel and their families; the selective service; and materials needed for defense. The committee is also responsible for investigating issues pertaining to defense policy in the U.S. Beneath the full committee are the Subcommittee on Airland, the Subcommittee on Emerging Threats and Capabilities, the Subcommittee on Personnel, the Subcommittee on Readiness and Management Support, the Subcommittee on Seapower, and the Subcommittee on Strategic Forces.

Commerce, Science, and Transportation Committee

There have been many predecessors to the Senate Standing Committee on Commerce, Science, and Transportation. The committee as it exists and is named today was previously known simply as the Committee on Commerce; the name was changed to its current name in 1977. Along with the change in name, the scope of the committee's jurisdiction was expanded. The standing committee and its subcommittees deal with the Coast Guard, coastal zone management, communications, highway safety, inland waterways, and interstate commerce. In addition, the committee addresses marine and ocean navigation, safety, and transportation, deepwater ports, marine fisheries, merchant marine and navigation, aeronautical and space sciences that are not military in nature, oceans, weather, and atmospheric activities, the Panama Canal and other canals that connect oceans, regulation of consumer products and services, regulation of interstate transportation, science, engineering, and technology R&D and policy, sports, standards and

measurement, transportation, and transportation and commerce aspects of Outer Continental Shelf lands.

Budget Committee

The Senate Standing Committee on the Budget was created in 1974. The Senate Standing Committee on the Budget has the responsibility for writing the annual Congressional budget plan and also for tracking actions related to the federal budget. The jurisdiction of the Senate Standing Committee on the Budget extends to oversight of the operation of the Congressional Budget Office. The purpose of the Senate Standing Committee on the Budget preparing the budget plan, also referred to as the budget resolution, is to lay out a general map for Congress with regard to the levels of government revenues and expenditures that are possible for the entire government. However, other Congressional Committees also draft legislation, and this legislation drafted by other committees is the legislation that enacts policies related to government spending and taxing.

Environment and Public Works Committee

The full Senate Standing Committee on Environment and Public Works has the responsibility for overseeing issues pertaining to biotechnology, the Council on Environmental Quality, Earth Day, the Convention on International Trade in Endangered Species, environmental conflict resolution, environmental education, environmental justice, the Environmental Protection Agency, environmental treaties, the Morris K. Udall Foundation for Scholarship and Excellence in National Environmental Policy, the National Environmental Education Act of 1969, the Noise Control Act of 1972, noise pollution, and nominations. There are a number of subcommittees of the Senate Standing

Committee on Environment and Public Works, including the Subcommittee on Transportation and Infrastructure, the Subcommittee on Clean Air, Climate Change, and Nuclear Safety, the Subcommittee on Fish, Wildlife, and Water, and the Subcommittee on Superfund and Waste Management.

Energy and Natural Resources Committee
The Committee on Energy and Natural Resources is the successor of the Committee on Public Lands, a very old Congressional committee, and therefore the jurisdiction of the committee has existed for nearly two hundred years. The name was changed from the Committee on Public Lands to the Committee on Energy and Natural Resources in 1977. The full committee has jurisdiction over energy policy, nuclear waste policy, privatization of federal government assets, territorial policy, issues pertaining to Native Hawaiian concerns, and ad hoc matters that include those which necessitate an expedited process, those which overlap the specialties of multiple subcommittees, and those which hold national importance. The Committee on Energy and Natural Resources has several subcommittees, including the Subcommittee on Energy, the Subcommittee on National Parks, the Subcommittee on Public Lands and Forests, and the Subcommittee on Water and Power.

Foreign Relations Committee
The Senate Standing Committee on Foreign Relations was created in 1816 as one of ten original Senate committees. The committee has jurisdiction over issues pertaining to acquiring property for U.S. embassies, U.S. boundaries, diplomatic service, foreign economic, military, technical, and humanitarian assistance, foreign loans, the Red Cross when it is operating internationally,

international matters related to nuclear energy, international conferences and congresses, international law, International Monetary Fund and other international monetary organizations, international intervention and war, efforts to foster U.S. commercial interests internationally, national security, ocean and international environmental and scientific matters, protection of U.S. citizens abroad, international relations, treaties, the United Nations, and the World Bank and other international development assistance organizations. Subcommittees include the Subcommittee on International Economic Policy, Export and Trade Promotion, the Subcommittee on Near Eastern and South Asian Affairs, the Subcommittee on European Affairs, the Subcommittee on East Asian and Pacific Affairs, the Subcommittee on African Affairs, the Subcommittee on Western Hemisphere, Peace Corps and Narcotics Affairs, and the Subcommittee on International Operations and Terrorism.

Finance Committee
The Senate Standing Committee on Finance has jurisdiction over issues pertaining to the debts of the United States, customs, collection districts, and ports, deposit of public money, general revenue sharing, health programs of the Social Security Act or funded by special taxes or trust funds, social security, reciprocal trade agreements, revenue measures, tariffs and import quotas, transportation of goods to which a duty is applied. The Senate Standing Committee on Finance has jurisdiction over the activities of a number of federal offices. The committee consists of several subcommittees, including the Subcommittee on Health Care, the Subcommittee on International Trade, the Subcommittee on Long-term Growth and Debt Reduction, the Subcommittee on Social Security and Family Policy, and the

Subcommittee on Taxation and IRS Oversight.

Homeland Security and Governmental Affairs Committee

The Senate Standing Committee on Homeland Security and Governmental Affairs has jurisdiction over issues pertaining to the Department of Homeland Security, the national archives, budget and accounting issues, the census and collecting statistics, Congressional organization, the Federal Civil Service, government information, intergovernmental relations, the District of Columbia, nuclear export policy, organization of the executive branch of the government, the postal service, and the status of officers and employees of the government. The subcommittees of the Senate Standing Committee on Homeland Security and Governmental Affairs include the Subcommittee on Federal Financial Management, Government Information, and International Security, the Permanent Subcommittee on Investigations, and the Subcommittee on Oversight of Government Management, the Federal Workforce and the District of Columbia.

Health, Education, Labor, and Pensions Committee

The Senate Standing Committee on Health, Education, Labor, and Pensions has jurisdiction over issues pertaining to education, labor, health, and public welfare, aging, agricultural colleges, the arts and humanities, biomedical research and development, child labor, convict labor, the Red Cross when it is operating within the U.S., equal employment opportunity, Gallaudet College, Howard University, and Saint Elizabeth's Hospital, handicapped people, labor standards, labor statistics, settling labor disputes, occupational safety and health, private pension plans, public health, railway labor and retirement, foreign laborers, student loans, wages and hours of labor. Subcommittees of the Senate Standing Committee on Health, Education, Labor, and Pensions include the Subcommittee on Retirement Security and Aging, the Subcommittee on Education and Early Childhood Development, the Subcommittee on Employment and Workplace Safety, and the Subcommittee on Bioterrorism and Public Health Preparedness.

Rules and Administration Committee

The Senate Standing Committee on Rules and Administration has jurisdiction over issues pertaining to the administration of the Senate Office Buildings the Senate branch of the Capitol Building, the rules and procedures that are used to organize Congress, Senate rules and regulations, corrupt activities, qualifications for Senators, federal elections, the government printing office and the printing of the Congressional record, Congressional meetings, attendance at Congressional meetings, use of funds from the Senate contingent fund, succession to the office of President, the procurement of books and manuscripts and the establishment of monuments and memorials, the Senate Library and artifacts in the Senate Office Buildings and in the Senate branch of the Capitol, services provided to the Senate, the U.S. Capitol and congressional office buildings, the Library of Congress, the Smithsonian, and the Botanic Gardens.

Judiciary Committee

The Senate Standing Committee on Judiciary was created in 1816 as one of ten original Senate committees. The Senate Standing Committee on Judiciary has broad jurisdiction in the Senate over many matters, including jurisdiction over the courts. The committee also has jurisdiction over antitrust policy and competition policy, the rights of consumers, the Constitution, civil rights, property rights. In addition the Senate Standing Committee on Judiciary has jurisdiction over matters pertaining to corrections and rehabilitation, matters involving criminal activities and drugs, immigration, border security, citizenship, intellectual property rights, terrorism, technology and homeland security.

Veterans Affairs Committee

The Senate Standing Committee on Veterans Affairs was established in 1970. The committee has jurisdiction over the compensation of veterans, the life insurance provided to veterans of the armed forces by the United States government, national cemeteries, the pensions of all wars of the United States, the acclimation of individuals who have served in the armed forces back into civilian life, civil relief for soldiers and sailors, the administration of veterans hospitals, medical care for veterans, in a broad sense all efforts made on behalf of veterans, and vocational training and educational services provided to veterans.

Small Business and Entrepreneurship Committee

The Senate Standing Committee on Small Business and Entrepreneurship was created in 1981 as the successor to the Select Committee on Small Business. The Senate Standing Committee on Small Business and Entrepreneurship has jurisdiction over the Small Business Administration. The Senate Standing Committee on Small Business and Entrepreneurship also has jurisdiction over legislation that is pertaining to other issues extending beyond those addressed by the Small Business Administration but that are requested to be investigated by the Senate Standing Committee on Small Business and Entrepreneurship. The Senate Standing Committee on Small Business and Entrepreneurship Study is also responsible for investigating topics of

concern to small businesses in the United States.

Select Committee on Ethics

The Senate Select Committee on Ethics has jurisdiction over issues pertaining to the Senate Code of Conduct. The committee implements the ethics program for the Senate, as each branch of the federal government has the responsibility of implementing its own ethics program. Each house of the legislative branch has its own ethics committee to implement its ethics program; the counterpart to the Senate Select Committee on Ethics is the House Committee on Standards of Official Conduct. Specifically, the Senate Select Committee on Ethics addresses issues involving the ethics and conduct of individuals associated with the Senate that are related to financial disclosure, gifts, travel reimbursements, honoraria bans, constraints on outside employment, conflicting interests, constraints on employment activities after serving the Senate, campaign activities, money for senate related business, mailings, employment practices, interventions with other government agencies, and annual budget limits.

Indian Affairs Committee

The Senate Committee on Indian Affairs was permanently established in 1984 after years as a temporary committee. The Senate Committee on Indian Affairs has jurisdiction over investigating the matters that pertain to the American Indian, Native Hawaiian, and Alaska Native populations in the United States. The committee also has jurisdiction to propose legislation that is aimed at relieving matters of difficulty for these populations. Some of the matters that have been addressed by the committee are education for Indian populations, economic development, land management, trust responsibilities, health care, and cases made by Indians against the U.S. government.

Special Committee on Aging

The Senate Special Committee on Aging was originally a temporary committee that was created in 1961, but it became a permanent committee in 1977. Because of its status as a special committee, it does not possess legislative authority. However, it can investigate matters of pertinence, and it does have the ability to oversee relevant programs. The Senate Special Committee on Aging addresses issues that are pertinent to older Americans. The committee provides the results of its investigations to the Senate and also makes legislative recommendations to the Senate. The committee also publishes documents that address public policies that are relevant to older Americans. The committee studies issues related to Medicare, pensions, and employment for older Americans. It also works to stop fraudulent activities that are aimed at the elderly.

Select Committee on Intelligence

The Senate Select Committee on Intelligence was established to investigate and to provide oversight of U.S. government intelligence activities and programs. The committee is responsible for conducting investigations and providing them to the Senate, which in turn can use the materials that were gathered in the investigations to generate legislative proposals. The committee is also responsible for providing reports to the Senate on U.S. government intelligence activities and programs. The committee is charged with ensuring that U.S. government agencies that are involved with intelligence activities provide information on intelligence that is required for the executive branch and the legislative branch to develop well-informed policies and to make good

decisions regarding national security. The committee also has the responsibility of providing oversight of U.S. government intelligence activities to make sure that they are consistent with and comply with the U.S. Constitution and laws.

Joint Committee on Taxation

The Joint Committee is made up of ten members. Five members are from the Senate Committee on Finance, three of which represent the majority and two which represent the minority; the remaining five members are from the House Committee on Ways and Means, and again three of these represent the majority and two represent the minority. The committee has a key role in the legislative process as it pertains to taxes. The committee investigates internal revenue taxes, efforts that could be made to simplify taxes, provides reports summarizing its investigations to the House Committee on Ways and Means and the Senate Committee on Finance and makes legislative recommendations, and reviews tax refunds that exceed two million dollars. The committee is required to provide a yearly report to Congress that lists refunds that exceed two million dollars, including the names of the individuals and businesses that are associated with these refunds and the exact amounts that are refunded.

Joint Committee on Printing

The Joint Committee on Printing has the responsibility of overseeing the activities of the United States Government Printing Office. In addition, the Joint Committee on Printing has jurisdiction and oversight over all of the printing processes and procedures that are used within the federal government. The Joint Committee on Printing must make sure that all federal government organizations and individuals who represent the federal government are acting in accordance with the laws that are relevant to printing, and it must also make sure that all government organizations and individuals representing the government comply with Government Printing and Binding Regulations.

Joint Economic Committee

The Joint Economic Committee was established in 1946 when Congress passed the Employment Act of 1946. It was one of two advisory committees established under the Employment Act of 1946. The other committee established under this act was the President's Council of Economic Advisers. The purpose of both of these committees is to study and investigate economic conditions and to make recommendations regarding possible efforts to better economic policy. The Joint Economic Committee is chaired by either a member of the Senate or a member of the House of Representatives; each time Congress convenes, the chair alternates between the two chambers of Congress.

Joint Committee on the Library

The Joint Committee on the Library is responsible for overseeing issues pertaining to the Library of Congress. The committee consists of five members each from both the Senate and the House of Representatives, for a total of ten members. Specifically, membership consists of the chair and four members of the Senate Committee on Rules and Administration, as well as the chair and four members of the Committee on House Administration. The seat of the chair is alternately held by a member of the House of Representatives or the Senate each time that Congress convenes. There are no subcommittees for the Joint Committee on the Library. The committee was created in 1802 for the

purpose of assisting with the expansion of a congressional library. Today, in addition to overseeing the Library of Congress, the committee also has jurisdiction over the art collection of Congress and the Botanic Garden. The committee can accept works of art on behalf of Congress and assign a spot in the U.S. Capitol to display the art.

A Bill

A bill is a piece of legislation that is formally introduces in Congress. A bill can originate in either the House of Representatives or in the Senate. When a bill originates in the House of Representatives it is designated as H.R. When a bill originates in the Senate it is designated by S. Bills are numbered in consecutive order. Bills can be categorized into either public bills or private bills. Public bills address general issues. If a public bill is both approved by Congress and signed by the President it is passed and it becomes a Public Law, or a Public Act. In contrast, private bills address individual circumstances. For example, private bills might be introduced to address a case against the Federal Government, immigration and naturalization cases, or land titles. If a private bill is both approved by Congress and signed by the President it is passed and it becomes a private law.

Bills for raising revenue, such as those for taxes, originate in the House of Representatives. All bills must pass both the Senate and the House of Representatives in the exact same form. A bill that passes in both houses is sent to the President, who can either sign the bill or veto it. If the President signs the Bill, it becomes law. If the President vetoes the bill, it is sent back to Congress, and if both the House and the Senate pass it by a two-thirds majority, the bill becomes law, thereby overriding the President's veto.

If the President neither vetoes a bill nor signs it within ten days after receiving it from Congress, it becomes a law without his signature. However, if Congress sends a bill to the President and then adjourns, it does not become law if the President does not sign the bill within ten days; this is known as a pocket veto.

New Law Process

Laws can originate in either the House of Representatives or the Senate. When a Congressman wants to propose a new law, that person sponsors the bill and introduces it to the respective Congressional chamber by either giving it to the clerk or placing it in a special box known as the hopper. A legislative number is assigned to the bill, designated by H.R. for bills originating in the House of Representatives or S. for bills originating in the Senate. The bill is printed and given to all members of the house. The bill is assigned to a committee for investigation and discussion, which often involves hearings.

Following an investigation into a proposed bill the committee either releases the bill and recommends that it be passed, recommends that the bill be revised prior to being released, or sets it aside so that it cannot be voted on. If a bill is released it is added to a calendar of bills waiting to be voted on. On the floor of the chamber the bill is read and if it passes by a simple majority it goes to the other Congressional house. In order for the bill to be introduced in the other house, a member of that house must announce the introduction of it. The same process of being assigned to a committee and investigation is repeated in the second house. If the bill also passes by a simple majority in the second house, it goes to a conference committee comprised of members of both houses.

The conference committee reconciles any differences between the two houses with regard to the bill and if any alterations are made the committee sends the bill back to each house for final approval. After the bill has been approved it is printed, or enrolled, and certified. The enrolled bill is the signed by both the Speaker of the House and the Vice President, who is the leader of the Senate. After the bill has received the necessary signatures, it is sent to the President of the United States, where he must sign it within ten days or veto it. If the President signs the bill it becomes law. If the President chooses to veto the bill, it is sent back to Congress, and if two-thirds of both houses vote to pass the bill, it becomes law without the President's signature.

Authorization and Appropriations

Authorization laws create, perpetuate, or alter federal programs, and they are required by House and Senate rules or laws before Congress can appropriate funds in the federal budget for the programs. Direct spending, also known as mandatory spending, involves expenditures for programs that are authorized by legislation that concurrently includes budget authority for the expenditures. Discretionary spending involves expenditures that are set annually by Congress. Discretionary spending is optional, as opposed to mandatory funding. An authorization can be permanent until Congress changes it, or an authorization can be applicable only in particular fiscal years. When an authorization expires, Congress can reauthorize the authorization through the legislative process. If an appropriations is made after the associated authorization expires it is referred to as an unauthorized appropriation.

Federal Government Powers

The national, or federal, government reserves powers that are not afforded to the states. The national government has the power to print money, the power to regulate business and commerce between states, the power to regulate business and commerce between the United States and other countries, the power to create treaties and to carry our foreign policies, the power to declare war, the power to maintain military forces, and the power to create post offices. The national government also has the power to create laws that are deemed essential to carrying out all of the other powers that are constitutionally granted to the national government.

Powers Denied and Restrictions on the Federal Government

There are a number of powers that the federal government is not granted. The federal government does not have the power to suspend the Writ of Habeas Corpus. The federal government does not have the power to pass a Bill of Attainder or an ex post facto law. The federal government is restricted from displaying preferential treatment for one state over others. The federal government does not have the power to spend money from the U.S. Treasury before first receiving the approval of Congress. The federal government does not have the power to confer a title of nobility to any individual. An individual who holds a federal government office is restricted from accepting gifts from foreign countries; this restriction exists to prevent offers that might constitute bribes.

Judicial Branch

The United States Judicial Branch was established with the creation of the U.S. Supreme Court, which was stipulated by Article III of the U.S. Constitution. The Supreme Court is the highest court in the United States and it is granted the judicial powers of the United States government. In addition to the Supreme Court, the judicial branch also consists of lower Federal courts that were created by Congress using its Constitutional powers. The responsibility of the Courts is to settle disputes about the meaning of laws and how laws are applied, and through judicial review to decide whether or not laws violate the U.S. Constitution. It is through judicial review that the judicial branch exercises the system of checks and balances with regard to the executive and legislative branches.

The Supreme Court

The Supreme Court is the highest court. The Supreme Court's is tasked with settling disputes involving the interpretation of the Constitution. The process of determining whether a law or action is in violation of the Constitution is judicial review. The Supreme Court can overturn both state and federal laws if they are determined to violate the Constitution. The decisions of the Supreme Court can only be altered by means of another Supreme Court decision or through an amendment to the Constitution. The Supreme Court has full authority over federal courts and restricted authority over state courts. The Supreme Court has the final say over cases heard by federal courts, and also stipulates the procedures that federal courts must abide by. Although federal courts are required to uphold the Supreme Court's interpretations of federal laws and the Constitution and the Supreme Court's interpretations of federal law and the Constitution also apply to state courts, the Supreme Court cannot interpret state laws or Constitutions and doesn't oversee state court procedures.

Supreme Court Justices

Nine Justices currently comprise the Supreme Court; eight of these are referred to as Associate Justices and one is referred to as the Chief Justice. The number of Supreme Court Justices is set by Congress. The Supreme Court Justices are appointed by the President of the United States and with consent from the Senate. After individuals have been approved by the Senate and have been sworn in to the Supreme Court, they may keep the position of Supreme Court Justice for the remainder of their lives. Justices may leave their positions if they choose to resign or retire, or if they die, or if they are impeached. Historically, there has never been a Justice who has been removed from the Supreme Court through impeachment. There are not any specific requirements to become a Supreme Court Justice.

Supreme Court Cases

The total number of cases sent to the Supreme Court annually is around 7,500. However, the Supreme Court typically only hears between eighty and one hundred of these cases. When a case is submitted to the Supreme Court, the Supreme Court Justices convene to determine whether the case should be heard before the Court. The criteria used to make this determination specifically include deciding whether the case addresses federal law or Constitutional law. In addition, the Justices must take into consideration the possibility that any decision made in the Supreme Court could affect the outcome of many cases heard before lower courts and subsequently make efforts to exercise this power only in cases involving a constitutional issue.

Supreme Court Hearing

The Supreme Court is in session from the first Monday in October through late June of the following year. If the Justices are not hearing cases, they conduct legal research and write opinions. On Fridays, Justices deliberate cases that they have heard and vote. If the Supreme Court Justices decide to hear a case, legal representation for each side has a half hour to present an oral argument. Justices may ask questions throughout oral arguments. A majority of the Justices are required to decide a case. If the Chief Justice sides with the majority, they write the majority opinion, or the Chief Justice assigns the task to another Justice on the majority side. If the Chief Justice does not side with the majority, the Justice who has served the longest on the Supreme Court writes the opinion or assigns the task to one of the other Justices. Opinions form the foundation for arguments in similar future cases, serving as precedent. Justices who are in the minority may write dissenting opinions.

The Supreme Court and Original Jurisdiction

Although it is rare for cases to originate in the Supreme Court, it does have the power of original jurisdiction to hear cases involving ambassadors and other foreign officials. Similarly, cases involving two or more states originate in the Supreme Court. If a decision made by a higher court is in disagreement with a decision made by a lower court, the decision made by the lower court is overturned. If a decision made by a higher court is in agreement with a decision made by a lower court, the losing party can request that the case be heard before the Supreme Court. However, only cases addressing federal or Constitutional law are heard before the Supreme Court.

Supreme Court Officers

The Supreme Court is aided by Court Officers, who help to ensure that the functions of the court are carried out smoothly. The Court Officers include the Administrative Assistant to the Chief Justice, who is appointed by the Chief Justice. In addition, the Court Officers include the Clerk, the Reporter of Decisions, the Librarian, and the Marshal, all of whom are appointed by the Supreme Court. The Court Officers also include the Director of Budget and Personnel, the Court Counsel, the Curator, the Director of Data Systems, and the Public Information Officer. These Court Officers are appointed by the Chief Justice with the advice of the rest of the Supreme Court.

Judicial Review

Courts possess the power of judicial review, which entails reviewing laws or official actions made on the part of government representatives to determine if those laws or actions are in violation of the Constitution. In the United State, the power of judicial review is held by courts. Specifically, the United States Supreme Court holds the highest power to make decisions regarding the constitutionality of both state and federal laws. The doctrine of judicial review was founded based on the decision of the Supreme Court in the case of Marbury v. Madison in 1803. In states, the power of judicial review lies with the highest appellate court, which can be referred to as a Supreme Court or the Court of Appeals.

Appealing Cases in Higher Courts

Prior to being heard before the Supreme Court, cases are typically first heard before lower courts, including both state and federal courts. If a lower court makes a decision that the losing party in the case believes is unjust, that party has the option of appealing the case and bringing it before a higher court. At the state level, courts where appeals are heard are referred to as appellate courts. At the federal level, lower courts are referred to as United States District Courts and higher courts are referred to as United States Courts of Appeals.

Federal Courts Jurisdiction

The Constitution stipulates that the federal courts have jurisdiction over cases involving a number of issues. Federal judicial power extends to cases involving the United States Constitution, federal laws and treaties. Federal courts deal with cases involving Ambassadors and other foreign officials, cases involving admiralty and maritime issues, cases in which the United States federal government is a party, cases involving disputes between two or more states, cases involving disputes between a state and citizens of another state, cases involving disputes between citizens of different states, cases involving citizens from one state who are claiming land in different states, and cases involving disputes between a state or its citizens and foreign states or foreign citizens. The Supreme Court has original jurisdiction in cases involving Ambassadors and other foreign ministers and in any case in which a state is a party. In all other cases, the Supreme Court has appellate jurisdiction.

Courts of Appeals

The second highest level of the federal judiciary branch is comprised of the courts of appeals. The courts of appeals were created in 1891 to reduce the overwhelming number of cases that were sent to the Supreme Court and more quickly and efficiently process cases. There are twelve regional circuit courts of appeal, as well as the U.S. Court of Appeals for the Federal Circuit. Most circuit courts have between ten and fifteen judges, but the number varies widely between courts. The purpose of the courts of appeals is to review the decisions of the district courts, or of the trial courts at the federal level, and to review orders of regulatory agencies in instances where the agencies have reviewed the orders themselves internally but there remains dissent over legal issues. The Court of Appeals for the Federal Circuit also has national jurisdiction to hear appeals in unique circumstances.

Special Courts

Occasionally a need arises to establish a court to meet a particular purpose. Such special courts are referred to as legislative courts, as they are established by Congress. In special courts judges are appointed to life terms, just as judges are in other federal courts. Also similarly to other federal court judges, special court judges must be appointed by the President of the U.S. and approved by the Senate. There are currently two special trial courts with national jurisdiction. The first is the Court of International Trade, which hears cases dealing with international trade and customs concerns. The second is the U.S. Court of Federal Claims, which hears cases involving claims for financial damages against the U.S. government, cases involving disputes concerning federal contracts, cases involving situations in which the federal government is accused of unlawfully taking private property, and other cases involving claims against the U.S government.

District Courts

The district courts are below the courts of appeals. There are ninety-four districts among the fifty states and territories of the U.S. Districts are established by Congress based on the population, the size, and the caseload in a particular area. Small states can represent an entire district; larger states are divided into up to four districts. There are at minimum two judges for every district court. Judges must be residents of the district they work in, with the exception of judges in D.C. District courts sessions are held in varying cities within a district for specific durations of time in each city. The types of cases that appear before district courts address issues related to federal crimes. District courts are the only federal courts in which a grand jury indicts individuals accused of criminal acts and a jury makes a decision on a case. In every district there is also a U.S. bankruptcy court, as bankruptcy issues must be handled in federal courts as opposed to state courts.

State and Local Courts

Every state has a court system that is independent and distinct from the federal court system. The hierarchy of the state court system includes trial courts at the lowest level; appellate courts are the highest courts in the state court system. The great majority, over ninety-five percent, of the court cases in the United States are heard and decided in state courts and local courts, which also fall under the jurisdiction of the states. Depending on the state, there may be one or two appellate courts within the state. States organize and name their courts differently. Typically, lower courts are assigned specific names and authority to hear specific types of cases, such as family courts and probate courts. Beneath the specialized trial courts are more informal trial courts, including magistrate courts and justice of the peace courts, which typically do not involve a jury.

State Court Judges

State court judges may take their seats in state courts in a number of ways. State judges can be appointed to state courts by a state governor. After a specific period of time has elapsed, these appointed judges may run in an election. State judges can also be initially elected to their seat in a state court, rather than first being appointed. Elections for judgeships are sometimes contested and partisan in nature. However, sometimes elections for these positions are not contested and not partisan in nature. States often try to better state and local judges by establishing pools of qualified legal professionals for state governors to select appointees from.

Police Powers of the State Courts

State courts have the authority to exercise what are referred to as police powers over specific issues. These issues include health, morals and safety. For example, in order to ensure the health or citizens, a state government can mandate that all children enrolled in school must receive vaccinations against particular diseases. If anyone wanted to challenge such a mandate issued under the police power of the state, they would have to do so in a state court. Police powers are granted by the tenth amendment of the United States Constitution. However, most state constitutions also include a Bill of Rights unique from the federal Bill of Rights that restricts the state's power over its citizens.

Appeals

If a case originates in a state court, it typically must be appealed within the state court system and have exhausted all possible appeal options within the state court system before it is possible to appeal the case within the federal court system. Also, in order for a case that has originated within the state court system to be appealed within the federal court system, the case must have something to do with a federal issue. If a decision is made by a state supreme court and the case involves a federal issue, it can be appealed to the U.S. Supreme Court. The U.S. Supreme Court then has the authority to overturn state laws.

State Government Powers

Each state government reserves the power to issue state licenses, the power to regulate business and commerce within the boundaries of the state, the power to hold elections, the power to create local governments, the power to ratify Constitutional amendments, and the power to regulate public health and safety. The state governments may also exercise powers that are not explicitly stipulated in the United States Constitution as being held by the federal government. Similarly, the state governments may exercise powers that the Constitution does not explicitly restrict the states from exercising.

Powers Denied to State Governments

There are a number of powers that are denied to state governments within the United States of America. These restrictions are stipulated by the Constitution of the United States. States are restricted from doing anything that the federal government is restricted from doing. States are also restricted from forming alliances or confederations. States are restricted from declaring war and maintaining navies. State governments are restricted from making and entering into treaties with foreign countries. In addition state governments are restricted from making money. State governments are also restricted from placing taxes on imports and exports from or to other states, respectively. States are restricted from preventing the requirements of a contract from being met as well. Finally, states are restricted from taking away an individual's rights without due process of law.

State vs. Federal Government

Initially, government systems in the United States were characterized as state governments that were essentially self-governed. These circumstances in the early days of the United States represented an aversion to the centralized government that was present in England, the colonial power that first controlled America. The state government system proved to be insufficient and therefore the Constitution was written to delineate the powers afforded to a federal government. The Constitution also delineates the relationship between the federal and state governments. The system instituted in the Constitution is a known as a federalist system, in which powers are shared between the federal and state governments. Specific powers are allocated to the federal government, while other powers remain in the hands of state governments.

Describe: Concurrent Powers

While both the national and state governments reserve specific powers that the other does not have, there are certain powers that are shared between the national and state governments. These shared powers are known as concurrent powers. The concurrent powers that are shared by both the national government and the state governments include the power to collect taxes, the power to build roads, the power to borrow money, the power to create courts, the power to create and enforce laws, the power to establish banks and corporations, the

power to spend funds in the interest of the general welfare of the United States and its citizens, and the power to take private property for purposes that benefit the public so long as just compensation is provided.

Powers Denied to Both the Federal Government and State Governments

There are a number of powers that are denied to both the federal government and state governments in the United States of America. These restrictions are stipulated by the Constitution of the United States. The federal government and state governments are restricted from conferring titles of nobility. Both levels of government are also restricted from allowing slavery to take place; this restriction is specifically stated in the thirteenth amendment of the United States Constitution. The federal and state governments are also restricted from prohibiting citizens of the United States from exercising their right to vote based on race, color, or based on previous conditions of servitude; this restriction is specifically stated in the fifteenth amendment of the United States Constitution. Finally, both the federal and state governments are also restricted from prohibiting citizens of the United States from exercising their right to vote based on gender; this restriction is explicitly stated in the nineteenth amendment of the United States Constitution.

State Constitutions

In the United States, state governments each have a unique state constitution. State constitutions resemble the federal Constitution in many ways. However, state constitutions may not be in disaccord with the federal Constitution. State governments have control over affairs that occur within state boundaries, such as communications within state boundaries, regulations concerning property, industry, business, and public utilities, criminal codes, and labor conditions. There are also numerous matters over which state and federal government shares jurisdiction. State constitutions differ from one another with regard to some issues, but typically they all are laid out similarly to the federal Constitution. All state constitutions contain a section on people's rights and a section that outlines how government should be organized. Every state constitution also stipulates that ultimate authority rests with the people and establishes specific standards and values as the basis of government.

State Executive and Legislative Branches

State governments are divided into executive, legislative, and judicial branches, just as in the federal government. In a state government, the governor serves as the head of the executive branch. The governor is elected by popular vote for a term of either two or four years depending on the state. Every state in the U.S. has a bicameral legislature except Nebraska, which has a single legislative body. The bicameral legislature is divided into an upper house and a lower house. The upper house is typically referred to as the Senate, as in the federal government, and the lower house can be referred to by a number of names, including the House of Representatives, the House of Delegates, or the General Assembly. State senators typically serve for a term of four years, while members of the House of Representatives, House of Delegates or the General Assembly serve for a term of two years.

State Legislatures

There are over seven thousand state legislators throughout the fifty states. Term limits exist for these legislatures in a number of states, but not all. There are also over thirty-five thousand staff members that have positions with state legislatures.

The organization and procedures of state legislatures serve as the foundation for state legislatures. Specifically, the key procedural components of state legislatures include parliamentary procedures; every state legislature establishes its own parliamentary procedures. Procedures also include those that are in place to effectively and efficiently operate committees; most legislatures have created personnel policies to organize the staff that carries out everything from research to security and from budgeting to technology support. State legislatures are organized at many levels in order to ensure that legislative staff members are working effectively and efficiently as well. One of the means of ensuring organization is through legislative sessions and session dates. Legislative sessions can be characterized as regular legislative sessions, which meet at regularly scheduled intervals, or as special or extraordinary legislative sessions, which are called by either the governor of a state or by the legislature itself with the purpose of addressing specific issues.

Tied Chambers in State Legislatures

A tied chamber occurs in a state legislature when the political parties represented in the legislature are equally divided. Usually, this is not the case. Normally, one political party has control over the state legislature. However, in recent times it has become more common for state legislative chambers to be divided equally along party lines. Such an equal division along party lines does not necessarily mean ensure that there will be a political deadlock within the state legislature. There are a number of methods that state legislatures use to move forward past a stalemate, including a coin toss, a vote by the lieutenant governor, statutory laws to guide legislatures through a deadlock situation, and negotiated agreements.

City Government

Approximately eighty percent of the population in the United States resides in urban areas or areas immediately surrounding urban areas. Therefore, city governments are an integral part of the general system of government within the United States. City governments provide direct services to their citizens even more so than the federal government or state governments. Examples of services that are provided by city governments include police forces and firefighting forces, health and sanitation, education, public transportation, and housing. City governments are chartered by state governments; the city charter outlines the objectives and powers allocated to the city. While many city governments operate independently from state governments, many large cities work in collaboration with state and federal government. The organization of city governments varies, but the majority have a central council that is chosen by the people through an election, as well as an executive officer who is aided by department heads. Traditionally, there are mayor-council city governments, commission city governments, and city manager city governments.

Mayor-Council City Governments

The mayor-council form of city government has existed the longest among the types of city governments in the United States. In a city where there is mayor-council form of government, there is a mayor who is elected by the people to serve as the chief executive officer for the city. There is also a city council that is elected by the people. The members of the city council represent the regions that make up the legislative branch. The mayor is responsible for appointing the people who head the numerous city departments. The mayor can also appoint other city officials. The mayor has the power to veto the laws of the city, which are also referred to as city ordinances. The mayor may also draft the budget for the city. The city council is responsible for passing the laws of the city, establishing city property taxes, and allocating funds among city departments.

City Manager City Governments

The city manager form of city government began in an effort to meet the needs of complicated issues that are common in modern day American cities. Meeting this complicated mix of issues requires experience and knowledge in a variety of matters, as well as managerial skills. Traditional elected officials do not always hold such skills, knowledge and expertise. To overcome this problem, some city governments have opted to have a single individual serve in the position of city manager, with the responsibility for exercising executive powers. City governments based on the city manager system have a relatively small city council that is chosen through election. This city council creates city ordinances and develops city policies. The city manager is hired by the city council to implement the laws and policies developed by the council. The city manager is also responsible for creating a city budget and overseeing city departments. There is typically no limit to the amount of time that an individual may serve in the position of city manager.

Commission City Governments

The commission form of city government represents a blending of the executive and legislative duties into one assembly of city officials known as the city commission. There are typically three or members of the city commission and they are chosen in a city-wide election. Every member of the city commission is charged with overseeing the responsibilities of at least one department of the city. One member of the city commission is selected to be the chairperson of the commission. The chairperson of the city commission is sometimes referred to as the mayor of the city. However, the chairperson of the city commission does not have any power above and beyond that of the other members of the city commission.

Town and Village Government

Many governments are too tiny to be classified as city governments. Such small jurisdictions are known as towns and villages and receive a charter from a state. Town and village governments address only local matters such as maintaining local roads, illuminating local roads, managing a local water supply, maintaining local police and firefighting forces, developing and implementing local health policies, providing or organizing the disposal of waste locally, setting local taxes, and managing local schools. Town and village governments are typically overseen by a board or a council that is chosen through election. A chairperson or a president can serve as the chief executive officer of the board or council. Alternatively, an elected mayor can serve as the chief executive officer of the board or council. Town and village governments can be staffed by clerks, treasurers, police and fire officers, and health and welfare officers.

County Government

A county is a sub region within a state. Counties typically consist of at least two towns and a number of villages. Usually a single city or town within a county is named as the county seat. The county seat serves as the site at which government offices are situated. The county seat is also where the board of commissioners for the county convenes. Small counties have boards which are selected by the entire county. In contrast, large counties have commissioners who represent each town, city or district within the county. County boards are responsible for setting county taxes, appropriating funds, setting pay rates for county personnel, overseeing county elections, building and upkeep of highways and bridges, and managing federal, state, and county social welfare programs.

Separation of Powers

Government at both the federal and state levels is characterized by a separation of powers. At the local level, the organization of government is different. State and local government often distinguishes between executive powers and law enforcement powers by allowing citizens to choose public prosecutors through elections. In some states citizens elect judges as well. In local governments, the election of individuals who represent special authority, such as police chiefs and members of school boards, serves to separate such individuals from the executive and legislative branches of government. At the local level, juries also have a significant role in maintaining the system of checks and balances, as they have the sole authority to determine the facts in most criminal and civil cases, restricting the power of the executive and judicial branches in enforcement of laws.

Town Meetings

Some local governments hold what are referred to as town meetings. Town meetings have occurred for more than two hundred years. The townships that hold town meetings are typically found throughout New England states. Town meetings are a rather unique characteristic that distinguishes some small town from other forms of government. Town meetings are typically held on an annual basis, but they can be held more often if necessary. At a town meeting, registered voters assemble in an open meeting to elect officers, discuss local matters, and vote on local legislation that concerns the operation of the local government. The attendees of the town meeting make decisions together as a community concerning issues such as road maintenance, building public facilities, tax rates, and town budgets.

Party Systems

There is a variety of party systems, including single-party systems, dominant-party systems, and dual-party systems. In a single-party system, only one political party may hold power. In this type of system, minor parties may be permitted, but they must accept the leadership of the dominant party. Dominant-party systems allow for multiple parties in opposition of one another, however the dominant party is the only party considered to have power. A two-party system, such as in the United States, is one in which there are two dominant political parties. In such a system, it is very difficult for any other parties to win an election. In most two-party systems, there is typically one right wing party and one left wing party.

Political Parties

A political party is an organization that advocates a particular ideology and seeks to gain power within government. The tendency of members of political parties to support their party's policies and interests relative to those of other parties is referred to as partisanship. Often, a political party is comprised of members whose positions, interests and perspectives on policies vary, despite having shared interests in the general ideology of the party. As such, many political parties will have divisions within them that have differing opinions on policy. Political parties are often placed on a political spectrum, with one end of the spectrum representing conservative, traditional values and policies and the other end of the spectrum representing radical, progressive value and policies.

Right-wing political parties in the United States of America are typically associated with conservatism or Christian democracy. Right-wing political parties and politics are considered to be the opposite of left-wing political parties and politics. In the United States of America, the Republican Party is the dominant right-wing political party. Left-wing political parties are typically associated with socialism, social democracy, or liberalism. Left-wing political parties and politics are considered to be the opposite of right-wing political parties and politics. In the United States of America, the Democratic Party is the dominant left-wing political party.

Two-Party System

Advocates of the two-party system argue that its advantages are that they are stable because they enable policies and government to change slowly rather than rapidly due to the relative lack of influence from small parties representing unconventional ideologies. In addition, they seem to drive voters towards a middle ground and are less susceptible to revolutions, coups, or civil wars. Among the critiques of the two-party system is the claim that stability in and of itself is not necessarily desirable, as it often comes at the expense of democracy. Critics also argue that the two-party system promotes negative political campaigns, in which candidates and their respective parties only take positions on issues that will differentiate themselves from their opponents, rather than focusing on policy issues that are of significance to citizens. Another concern is that if one of the two major parties becomes weak, a dominant-party system may develop.

Republican Party

The Republican Party is often referred to as the GOP, which stands for Grand Old Party. The Republican Party is considered socially conservative and economically neoliberal relative to the Democratic Party. Like the Democratic Party, there are factions within the Republic Party that agree with the party's overall ideology, but disagree with the party's positions on specific issues. The official symbol of the Republican Party is the elephant. The Republican National Committee (RNC) is the official organization of the Republican Party, and it develops and promotes the party's platform and coordinates fundraising and election strategies. There are Republican committees in every U.S. state and most U.S. counties.

Democratic Party

The Democratic Party was founded in 1792. In the United States, it is one of the two dominant political parties, along with the Republican Party. The Democratic Party is to the left of the Republican Party. The Democratic Party began as a conservative party in the mid-1800s, shifting to the left during the 1900s. There are many factions within the

Democratic Party in the United States. The Democratic National Committee (DNC) is the official organization of the Democratic Party, and it develops and promotes the party's platform and coordinates fundraising and election strategies. There are Democratic committees in every U.S. state and most U.S. counties. The official symbol of the Democratic Party is the donkey.

Green Party

The Green Party is a liberal minority party that has been in existence since the 1980s. However, it was not until the presidential campaigns of 1996 and 2000, when Ralph Nader ran as the presidential nominee on the Green Party ticket, that the party gained widespread recognition. Members of the Green Party have won elections predominantly at the local level in the United States, and typically in nonpartisan-ballot elections where candidates were not identified on the ballot as having an affiliation with a political party. The Green Party advocates decentralization of government and local autonomy. There are ten core values held by the Green Party, which are based on the four pillars of the Green Party in Europe. These are community-based economics; decentralization; ecological wisdom; feminism; grassroots democracy; non-violence; personal and global responsibility; respect for diversity; social justice; and sustainability.

Constitution Party

The Constitution Party is a conservative minority party in the U.S. that was originally founded as the U.S. Taxpayers Party in 1992; its name was changed in 1999. The Constitution Party represents the third largest percentage of registered voters in the U.S. Members believe that U.S. laws originate from the Bible, take a

- 48 -

very conservative approach to social issues such as homosexuality and abortion and push for a more prominent role of religion in the lives of U.S. citizens. Members also support a stricter conformity to what they interpret as the original intent of the U.S. Constitution and the principles of the Declaration of Independence. The Constitution Party supports limiting federal government by reducing taxes, regulations and spending, particularly social programs such as welfare, education and healthcare. The party is also opposed to U.S. involvement in international affairs, illegal immigration and governmental welfare, and interprets the Second Amendment as securing the individual right to own guns.

Reform Party

The Reform Party of the United States of America is a minority party that was founded in 1995 by Ross Perot out of the belief that U.S. citizens were disillusioned with politics and wanted an alternative to the two dominant parties. Some of the issues that formed the platform of the Reform Party were financial reform issues including the federal deficit and national debt, government reform issues such as term limits, campaign finance reform, and lobbying reform, and trade issues. The Reform Party advocates maintaining a balanced budget, campaign finance reform, responsible immigration enforcement, opposition to free trade agreements like NAFTA, withdrawal from the WTO, limiting social welfare programs, and term limits for U.S. Representatives and Senators.

Libertarian Party

The Libertarian Party is a minority party that was created in 1971 out of the belief that the two dominant parties in the U.S. had deviated from the libertarian principles of the American founding

fathers. The core value of the Libertarian Party is individual liberty. The Libertarian Party advocates for limiting government, an end to taxes, a minimally regulated free market economy, the right to keep and bear arms, drug legalization, abolishment of the government social welfare system, civil liberties, a foreign policy of free trade and non-intervention, and the right to abortion. The party opposes the use of military force to achieve goals, as well as any form of gun control.

Political Campaigns

A political campaign is an organized attempt to influence the decisions of a particular group of people . Examples of campaigns could include elections or efforts to influence policy changes. One of the first steps in a campaign is to develop a campaign message. The message must then be delivered to the individuals and groups that the campaign is trying to reach and influence through a campaign plan. There are various ways for a campaign to communicate its message to the intended audience, including public media; paid media such as television, radio and newspaper ads, billboards and the internet; public events such as protests and rallies; meetings with speakers; mailings; canvassing; fliers; and websites. Through these efforts, the campaign attempts to attract additional support and, ultimately, to reach the goal of the campaign.

Political campaigns consist of three main elements, which are the campaign message, the money that is necessary to run the campaign and "machine", or the capital that is necessary run the campaign. A campaign message is a succinct statement expressing why voters should support the campaign and the individual or policy associated with that campaign. The message is one of the most significant aspects of a political campaign, and a considerable amount of time, money and effort is invested in devising a successful campaign message, as it will be repeated throughout the campaign and will be one of the most identifying factors of the campaign.

Political campaigns in the U.S. have changed and continue to change as advances in technology permit varied campaign methods. Campaigns represent a civic practice, and today they are a high profit industry. The U.S. has an abundance of professional political consultants that employ highly sophisticated campaign management strategies and tools. The election process varies widely between the federal, state and local levels. Campaigns are typically controlled by individual candidates, rather than by the parties that they are associated with. Larger campaigns utilize a vast array of media to reach their targeted audiences, while smaller campaigns are typically limited to direct contact with voters, direct mailings and other forms of low-cost advertising to reach their audiences. In addition to fundraising and spending done by individual candidates, party committees and political action committees also raise money and spend it in ways that will advance the cause of the particular campaign they are associated with.

Money is a significant aspect of a campaign because with changes in technology, campaigns have become increasingly expensive to run. Some of the costs associated with running a campaign include TV advertisements, mailings, and campaign staff salaries. Fundraising is often used to generate money to cover campaign costs. The capital that is necessary to run a campaign refers to human capital, which may consist of paid staff, volunteers, or a combination of both. Key members of a campaign include a campaign manager, people to make strategic decisions, and people to canvass door-to-door and make phone calls.

Political Campaign Staff

The staff employed by a political campaign receive a salary in exchange for their efforts to devise and implement a strategy for a successful campaign. Campaigns are typically led by a campaign manager. Beneath the campaign manager are department directors. The various departments in a political campaign can include the field department, the communications department, the finance department, the compliance and legal departments, the technology department, and the scheduling and advance department, which sends people to events in advance of a candidate to ensure that the details of the event are in order. Beneath the department level, campaign structure varies widely. On larger campaigns, there may be multiple coordinators each serving a particular function within individual departments. Interns and volunteers represent the bottom tier of the campaign, and they perform the necessary, but tedious, tasks of the campaign.

Canvassing

Canvassing is a method used to solicit votes from people that enables a political campaign to speak with a large number of individuals. The goals of canvassing efforts are to try to convince voters to vote for a candidate, to increase recognition of a candidate's name, and to generate supporters. Canvassing can take one of two forms: field canvassing and phone canvassing. Field canvassing is done door to door, approaching every residence in a voting district. This method typically enables canvassers to speak with an increased number of people, who are generally more inclined to speak with someone in person than over the phone, and also enables canvassers to distribute literature and put up lawn signs. Sometimes the candidate will also conduct field canvassing efforts. Phone canvassing is typically done using a phone bank, and therefore can reach even more people than field canvassing efforts. Phone canvassing is particularly useful in rural areas. However, many individuals are not receptive to unsolicited phone calls, which they associate with telemarketing.

Voting Systems

Different types of voting systems exist in the United States of America. In a single vote system, the voter can only vote for one option, precluding the voter from voting for anyone else. Alternatively, in a multiple vote system, the voter may vote for multiple options. In a ranked vote system, a voter may rank alternative options in order of preference. In a scored, or rated, vote system, the voter gives each option a score that falls on a scale between one and whatever number represents the upper boundary of the scale.

Voting

Voting is a method of decision making that allows people to express their opinion or preference for a candidate or for a proposed resolution of an issue. In a democratic system, voting typically takes place as part of an election. An individual participates in the voting process by casting a vote, or a ballot; ballots are produced by states A secret ballot can be used at polls to protect voters' privacy. Individuals can also vote via absentee ballot. In some states voters can write-in a name to cast a vote for a candidate that is not on the ballot. Some states also use

straight ticket voting, allowing the voter to vote for one party for all the elected positions on the ballot.

Voter Eligibility

The United States Constitution establishes that individual people are permitted to vote in elections if they are citizens of the United States and are at least eighteen years old. The fifteenth and nineteenth amendments of the United States Constitution stipulate that the right to vote cannot be denied to any United States citizen based on race or sex, respectively. States regulate voter eligibility beyond the minimum qualifications stipulated by the United States Constitution. Depending on the regulations of individual states, individuals may be denied the right to vote if they are convicted criminals.

Elections

In the United States, officials are elected at the federal, state and local levels. The first two articles of the Constitution, as well as various amendments, establish how federal elections are to be held. The President is elected indirectly, by electors of an electoral college. Members of the electoral college nearly always vote along the lines of the popular vote of their respective states. Members of Congress are directly elected. At the state level, state law establishes most aspects of how elections are held. There are many elected offices at the state level, including a governor and state legislature. There are also elected offices at the local level.

Presidential Elections

The President of the United States is elected indirectly, by members of an electoral college. Members of the electoral college nearly always vote along the lines of the popular vote of their respective states. The winner of a presidential election is the candidate with at least 270 Electoral College votes. It is possible for a candidate to win the electoral vote, and lose the popular vote. Incumbent Presidents and challengers typically prefer a balanced ticket, where the President and Vice President are elected together and generally balance one another with regard to geography, ideology, or experience working in government. The nominated Vice Presidential candidate is referred to as the President's running mate.

Voter Registration

Individuals have the responsibility of registering to vote. Every state except North Dakota requires citizens to register to vote. In an effort to increase voter turnout, Congress passed the National Voter Registration Act in 1993. The Act is also known as "Motor Voter", because it required states to make the voter registration process easier by providing registration services through drivers' license registration centers, as well as through disability centers, schools, libraries, and mail-in registration. Some states are exempt because they permit same-day voter registration, which enables voters to register to vote on the day of the election.

Congressional Elections

Congressional elections are every two years. Members of the House of Representatives are elected for a two year term and elections occur every two years on the first Tuesday after November 1st in even years. A Representative is elected from each of 435 House districts in the U.S. House elections usually occur in the same year as Presidential elections. Members of the Senate are elected to six year terms; one-third of the Senate is elected every two years. Per the Seventeenth Amendment to the Constitution, which was passed in 1913, Senators are elected by the electorate of states. The country is divided into Congressional districts, and critics argue that this division eliminates voter choice, sometimes creating areas in which Congressional races are uncontested. Every ten years redistricting of Congressional districts occurs. However, redistricting is often partisan and therefore reduces the number of competitive districts. The division of voting districts resulting in an unfair advantage to one party in elections is known as gerrymandering. Gerrymandering has been criticized as being undemocratic.

Electoral College

Electoral College votes are cast by state by a group of electors; each elector casts one Electoral College vote. State law regulates how states cast their Electoral College votes. In all states except Maine and Nebraska, the candidate winning the most votes receives all the state's electoral college votes. In Maine and Nebraska two electoral votes are awarded based on the winner of the statewide election, and the rest go to the highest vote-winner in each of the state's congressional districts. Critics of the Electoral College argue that it is undemocratic because the President is elected indirectly as opposed to directly, and that it creates inequality between voters in different states because candidates focus attention on voters in swing states who could influence election results. Critics argue that the Electoral College provides more representation for voters in small states than large states, where more voters are represented by a single electoral than in small states and discriminates against candidates that do not have support concentrated in a given state.

State and Local Elections

State elections are regulated by state laws and constitutions. In keeping with the ideal of separation of powers, the legislature and the executive are elected separately at the state level, as they are at the federal level. In each state, a Governor and a Lieutenant Governor are elected. In some states, the Governor and Lieutenant Governor are elected on a joint ticket, while in other states they are elected separately from one another. In some states, executive positions such as Attorney General and Secretary of State are also elected offices. All members of state legislatures are elected, including state senators and state representatives. Depending on the state, members of the state supreme court and other members of the state judiciary may be chosen in elections. Local government can include the governments of counties and cities. At this level, nearly all government offices are filled through an election process. Elected local offices may include sheriffs, county school boards, and city mayors.

Campaign Finance

Running a campaign requires money, however the means of funding campaigns is often controversial. Both individuals and organizations donate significant private contributions to campaigns. Money donated to campaigns can be characterized as either hard money and soft money. Hard money is contributed directly to a campaign. Soft money is not contributed directly to a campaign and is not legally coordinated by the official campaign itself; it is, however, spent to fund efforts that benefit the candidate, such as advertising. The administration and enforcement of campaign finance law is the responsibility of the Federal Election Commission, which was created in 1975.

An individual or group is legally permitted to make unlimited independent expenditures in association with federal elections. An independent expenditure is an expenditure that is made to pay for a form of communication that supports the election or defeat of a candidate; the expenditure must be made independently from the candidate's own campaign. To be considered independent, the communication may not be made with the cooperation or consultation with, or at the request or suggestion of, any candidate, any committees or political party associated with the candidate, or any agent that acts on behalf of the candidate. There are no restrictions on the amount that anyone may spend on an independent expenditure, however, any individual making an independent expenditure must report it and disclose the source of the funds they used.

Political parties participate in federal elections at the local, state and national levels. Most party committees must register with the Federal Election Committee and file reports disclosing federal campaign activities. While party committees may contribute funds directly to federal candidates, the amounts that they contribute are restricted by the campaign finance contribution limits. National and state party committees are permitted to make additional coordinated expenditures, within limits, to assist their nominees in general elections. However, national party committees are not permitted to make unlimited independent expenditures to support or oppose federal candidates using soft money. State and local party committees are also not permitted to use soft money for the purpose of supporting or opposing federal candidates, but they are allowed to spend soft money, up to a limit of $10,000 per source, on voter registration and on efforts aimed at increasing voter participation. All party committees are required to register themselves and file disclosure reports with the Federal Election Committee once their federal election activities exceed specified monetary limits.

Campaign Finance Disclosure

Campaign finance law mandates that candidate committees, party committees and PACs must file reports disclosing the money that they fundraise and spend. Federal candidate committees must disclose all PACs and party committees that donate money to them; the names, occupations, employers and addresses of all individuals who donate more than $200 in an election cycle; and all expenditures greater than $200 per election cycle for services rendered by an individual or vendor. States and local candidates are also mandated to disclose donations from PACs and party committees. It is becoming commonplace for campaign finance statements to be filed electronically.

Federal Election Campaign Act

In 1974, Congress passed the Federal Election Campaign Act, requiring candidates to disclose sources of campaign contributions and expenditures. The Act was amended to limit campaign contributions. The act limited individual contributions to one thousand dollars per campaign, banned direct contributions from corporations and trade unions, and limited contributions from political action committees, known as PACs, to five thousand dollars per campaign. A PAC is a private group that is organized on behalf of a special interest to aid in efforts to elect or defeat political candidates; the overriding goal of a PAC is to support candidates who would further legislation that is in the interest of the special interest. The number of PACs in the U.S.

exceeds four thousand due to the increase in the creation of PACs in response to the ban on campaign contributions from corporations and trade unions. The Federal Election Campaign Act introduced public funding for Presidential primaries and elections and called for the creation of the Federal Election Committee, which administers campaign finance law.

Bipartisan Campaign Reform Act

In 2002, Congress passed the Bipartisan Campaign Reform Act. The act made it illegal for local and national parties to spend soft money and for national party committees to accept or spend soft money; it increased the limit placed on individual campaign contributions from $1,000 to $2,000; it banned corporations or trade unions from contributing to issue advertising directly; and it made it illegal for corporations or trade unions to fund advertisements that mention a federal candidate within 60 days of a general election or within 30 days of a primary.

Primaries and Caucuses

Candidates for federal office are chosen by primaries and caucuses. In a primary election, voters in a jurisdiction choose a political party's candidate for a later election. Candidate for state level offices are also selected through primaries. The purpose of a caucus is also to nominate candidates for a later election. A caucus is a meeting that takes place in a precinct with the purpose of discussing each party's platform and voting issues such as voter turnout. Eleven states hold caucuses. The period of time known as the primary season in Presidential elections, which includes both primaries and caucuses, lasts from the Iowa caucus in January to the last primary, ends in early summer.

Front Loading and Invisible Primaries

Sometimes too many primaries take place early in the primary season, resulting in a reduction in the number of realistic Presidential candidates because campaign donors to withdraw their support for those candidates that are not viewed as viable options; this is called front loading. The candidates that are most successful in their run for office are not always the candidates who do well in the early primaries. Some candidates attempt to generate support, funding, and media coverage prior to the start of the official primaries in what is referred to as the invisible primaries.

Survey Sampling

Survey sampling is a method that involves the random selection of a sample from a population that is fixed in size. Survey sampling is often used to measure public opinion. The simplest method of survey sampling is referred to as simple random sampling. Simple random sampling makes sure that each and every possible subset of the defined population which has the desired sample size is given the same probability of being selected. Another method of survey sampling is stratified sampling. In addition, cluster sampling and multistage sampling represent other methods of survey sampling.

Public Opinion

Public opinion represents the collective attitudes of individual members of the adult population in the United States of America. There are many varied forces that may influence public opinion. These forces include public relations efforts on the part of political campaigns and political parties. Another force affecting political opinion is the political media and the mass media. Public opinion is very

important during elections, particularly Presidential elections, as it is an indicator of how candidates are perceived by the public and of how well candidates are doing during their election campaigns. Public opinion is often measured and evaluated using survey sampling.

Mass Media and Public Opinion

The mass media is critical in developing public opinion. In the short term people generally evaluate information they receive relative to their own beliefs; in the long term the media may have a considerable impact on people's beliefs. Due to the impact of the media on an individual's beliefs, some experts consider the effects of the media on an individual's independence and autonomy to be negative. Others view the impact of the media on individuals as a positive one, because the media provides information that expands worldviews and enriches life, and fosters the development of opinions that are informed by many sources of information. A critical aspect of the relationship between the media and public opinion is who is in control of the knowledge and information that is disseminated through the media. Whoever controls the media can propagate their own agenda. The extent to which an individual interprets and evaluates information received through the media can influence behaviors such as voting patterns or consumer behavior, as well as social attitudes.

Political Media

The political media includes forms of the media that are owned and overseen and managed by, or influenced by, political entities. The purpose of the political media is to disseminate the views and platforms of the associated political entity. The media is often referred to as a fourth power, in addition to the executive, legislative and judicial branches of the government. The internet is considered by some to be a form of political media. However, the internet is not completely identifiable as a political medium, given the lack of a central authority and the lack of a common political method of communication via the internet.

Protest

A protest is an expression of opposition, and sometimes of support, to events or circumstances. Protests represent a means for individuals to publicly make their views heard in an effort to influence public opinion or government policy, or a means to enact change. Protests generally result when self expression of opposing views is restricted by government policy, political or economic circumstances, religion, social structures, or the media, and people react by declaring their views through cultural mechanisms or on the streets. There are numerous forms of protest, including boycotts, civil disobedience, demonstrations, non-violent protests, picketing, protest marches, protest songs, riots, sit-ins, teach-ins, strikes, and others.

Petition

A petition is a request to an authority, most commonly a government official or public office or agency. A petition typically takes the form of a document that is addressed to an official who holds authority and that is signed by multiple individuals. In addition to written petitions, people may submit oral petitions, and today petitions are often internet-based. The First Amendment to the U.S. Constitution contains a clause known as the Petition Clause, which guarantees the right "to petition the Government for a redress of grievances." The right to petition includes the right to file lawsuits against the government.

Petitions can be used for many purposes. One example includes petitions to qualify candidates for public office to appear on a ballot; in order for a candidate's name to appear on a ballot, the candidate must collect signatures from voters. Other types of petitions include those used in efforts to generate support for various causes.

Special Interest Groups

A special interest group is a political organization that is created to influence policy or legislators involved in a particular policy area. Special interest groups could include corporations, trade associations, trade unions, senior citizens or individuals with disabilities, or even groups within the legislature or bureaucracy. The goal of special interest groups is to attempt to influence government. There are two types of special interest groups, including protective groups and promotional groups. Protective groups represent one part of society, for example professional organizations, veterans' organizations and trade unions. Membership in protective groups is limited to individuals who are members of the organizations representing the specific part of society they do. In contrast, promotional groups advocate a greater cause and claim to represent the common interests of humankind. Examples of promotional groups include Greenpeace and Friends of the Earth. Membership in promotional groups is open to all individuals, and as such are much larger than protective groups.

Comparative Politics

Anarchism

Anarchism is a philosophy that is synonymous with anti-authoritarianism. Many people wrongly associate anarchism with chaos, but in fact anarchists embrace political philosophies and social movements that support the abolition of government and social hierarchy. In a system that is based on anarchism, political and economic institutions would not exist. Rather, individual and community relationships would be voluntary, and people would strive towards a society based on autonomy and freedom. On the one hand, anarchists oppose coercive institutions and social hierarchies, and on the other they advocate a positive conception of how a voluntary society could work. As with many political ideologies, there are many factions that fall under the umbrella of anarchism that hold varying opinions of how anarchism should be defined. For instance, some anarchists support the use of violence to promote their ideology, while others do not.

Representative Democracy

In a system of government characterized as a representative democracy, voters elect representatives to act in their interests. Typically, a representative is elected by and responsible to a specific subset of the total population of eligible voters; this subset of the electorate is referred to as a representative's constituency. A representative democracy may foster a more powerful legislature than other forms of government systems; to compensate for a strong legislature, most constitutions stipulate that measures must be taken to balance the powers within government, such as the creation of a separate judicial branch. Representative democracy became popular in post-industrial nations where increasing numbers of people expressed an interest in politics, but where technology and census counts remained incompatible with systems of direct democracy. Today, the majority of the world's population resides in representative democracies, including constitutional monarchies that possess a strong representative branch.

Totalitarianism

Totalitarianism is a form of authoritarian political system in which the government regulates practically every aspect of public and private conduct. Under totalitarianism, individuals and institutions are enveloped into the state's ideology, and the government imposes its political authority by exercising absolute and centralized control over all aspects of life. Individuals are subordinate to the state, and opposition to political and cultural expression is suppressed. Totalitarian regimes do not tolerate activities by individuals or groups that are not geared toward achieving the state's goals and maintaining the state's ideology. A totalitarian regime maintains power via the use of secret police, propaganda disseminated through government controlled media, regulation and restriction of free speech, and use of terror tactics.

Authoritarianism

Authoritarian regimes enforce strong, even oppressive, measures against individuals that fall within their sphere of influence; they often arise when a governing body presumes that it knows what is right for a nation and enforces it. They are typically led by an elite group that employs repressive measures to maintain power, and they do not generally make efforts to gain the consent of individuals or permit feedback on their policies. Under an authoritarian government, people are often subject to government control over aspects of their lives that in many other systems would be considered personal matters. There is a spectrum of authoritarian ideologies. Examples of authoritarian regimes include absolute monarchies and dictatorships. Democracies can also exhibit authoritarian characteristics in some situations, such as efforts to promote national security. Authoritarian governments typically extend broad-reaching powers to law enforcement bodies, sometimes resulting in a police state; they may or may not have a rule of law, and are often corrupt.

Fascism

Fascism is an authoritarian political ideology and defined the form of rule in Italy from 1922 to 1943 under the leadership under Mussolini. Fascism is characterized by efforts to exert state control over all aspects of life, to hold the nation and political party above the individual, and to hold the state as supreme. Fascism also emphasizes loyalty to a single leader, and submission to a single nationalistic culture. Fascists support corporatism as an economic system, in which economic and social interests of diverse individuals are combined with the interests of the state.

Communism

Communism is a form of an authoritarian, or in some cases totalitarian, political system. A communist country is governed by a single political party that upholds the principles of Marxism-Leninism. The goal of communism is to dissolve the state into a classless society. According to Marxism, a communist state

is one in which the resources and means of production are communally owned rather than individually owned and which provides for equal sharing of all freedoms, work and benefits. Marxism argues that socialism is a necessary intermediate phase in achieving communism. Therefore, states that are governed by a communist party are actually socialist states, and not true communist states, since a true communist state could not exist given the goal of elimination of the state. Historically, communist states have often arisen during political instability. Within communist states there have rarely been restrictions on state power, resulting in state structures which are totalitarian or authoritarian. Marxist-Leninist ideology views any restriction on state power as an interference in the goal of reaching communism.

Monarchy

Monarchy, or rule by a single individual, is one of the oldest forms of government and is defined as an autocratic system in which a monarch serves as Head of State. In such a system, the monarch holds office for life. Also included in a monarchy are the individuals and institutions that comprise the royal establishment. In elective monarchies, monarchs are appointed to their position for life; in most instances, elective monarchies been succeeded by hereditary monarchies. In a hereditary monarchy, the title of monarch is inherited according to a line of succession; typically one family can trace its origin along a dynasty or bloodline. Most monarchs represent merely a symbol of continuity and statehood, rather than actually serving as a participant in partisan politics. The practice of choosing a monarch varies between countries. A constitutional monarchy is one in which the rule of succession is typically established by a law passed by a representative body.

Autocracy, Absolutism, Despotism and Dictatorship

Autocracy is a form of a political system in which unlimited power is held by a single person. Absolutism is a form of autocratic political system. Absolutists believe that one person should hold all power. Historically, a monarch ruled in a system characterized as absolutist. Some people believed that an absolute ruler was chosen by God; in this case opposition against the monarch was equivalent to opposition to God. Therefore, rule was considered absolute in the sense that the ruler could not be challenged. Despotism is another form of autocratic political system, characterized as having a government overseen by a single authority that wields absolute power; the authority could be either an individual or a group. A dictatorship is a form of absolute rule by a leader, referred to as a dictator, who is unrestricted by law, constitutions, or other social and political forces. Dictatorships are typically associated with single-party states, military regimes, and other forms of authoritarianism.

Democracy

Democracy, or rule by the people, is a form of government in which power is vested in the people and in which policy decisions are made by the majority in a decision-making process such as an election that is open to all or most citizens. Definitions of democracy have become more generalized and include aspects of society and political culture in democratic societies that do not necessarily represent a form of government. What defines a democracy varies, but some of the characteristics of a democracy could include the presence of a middle class, the presence of a civil society, a free market, political pluralism, universal suffrage, and specific rights and freedoms. In practice however, democracies do have limits on specific freedoms, which are justified as being necessary to maintain democracy and ensure democratic freedoms. For example, freedom of association is limited in democracies for individuals and groups that pose a threat to government or to society.

PatriarchyTyranny

A patriarchy is a form of autocratic system in which the male members of society tend to hold positions of power. In such a system, the more powerful a position is, the more likely it is that a male will hold that position. Patriarchy also describes systems that are characterized as having male leadership in certain hierarchical churches or religious bodies. Tyranny is also a form of autocratic system, in which an individual described as a tyrant possesses and wields absolute power and rules by tyranny. Tyrants are typically characterized as cruel despots that place greater significance on their own interests or the interests of a small group of individuals than on the interests of the population and the state that they govern.

Parliamentary System

A parliamentary system is a representative democratic system in which the executive branch of government is dependent on the support of a parliament. In this system, there is no obvious separation of powers between the executive and legislative branches. However, parliamentary systems are generally flexible and responsive to the public. They are characterized as having both a head of government, who is typically the prime minister, and a head of state, who is often a symbol possessing only ceremonial powers. Some parliamentary systems also have an elected president. The features of a parliamentary system include an executive cabinet, headed by the head of government. The cabinet can be removed by the parliament by a vote of no confidence, and likewise the parliament can be dissolved by the executive.

Westminster System

The Westminster System is a form of representative democracy, modeled after the system used in the United Kingdom's Palace of Westminster, where the UK Parliament is located. Features of the Westminster system include an executive branch comprised of members of the legislature; a Cabinet made up of senior members of the executive branch; the existence of opposition parties; an elected legislature, or a system comprised of two houses, one of which is elected and the other of which is appointed; and a ceremonial head of state, who is distinct from the head of government, and who may hold reserve powers that are not usually exercised. Members of parliament are elected by popular vote, and the head of government is selected via an invitation from the head of state to establish an administration. The head of government, referred to as the Prime Minister, must control a majority of seats within the lower house of parliament or must ensure that there is no absolute majority against them.

Oligarchy

Oligarchy, or rule by the few, is a form of political system in which the majority of political power is held by a small portion of society. This power usually resides with the most powerful individuals or groups, such as those that possess wealth, military might, or political influence. Oftentimes, oligarchies are comprised of a few powerful families, in which power is passed on from one generation to the next. Members of oligarchies may not wield their power openly, but may instead exercise power from behind the scenes, particularly through economic measures.

Presidential/Congressional System

In a presidential system, also referred to as a congressional system, the legislative branch and the executive branches are elected separately from one another. The features of a presidential system include a president who serves as both the head of state and the head of the government, who has no formal relationship with the legislative branch, who is not a voting member, who cannot introduce bills, and who has a fixed term of office. Elections are held at scheduled times. The president's cabinet carries out the policies of the executive branch and the legislative branch.

Republic

A republic is a state in which supreme power rests with citizens who vote to elect representatives to be responsible to them. The organization of government in a republic can vary. In most republics the head of state is referred to as the President, and in a democratic republic the head of state is chosen in an election. In some countries the constitution restricts the number of terms that an individual can serve as president. In the United States, where the head of state is also the head of government, the system is known as a presidential system.

Aristocracy, Meritocracy and Plutocracy

Aristocracy is a form of oligarchic system in which the government is led by a ruling class that is considered, either by themselves or by others, to be superior to other members of society. Meritocracy,

- 60 -

or rule by those who most deserve to rule, is a system that is more flexible than an aristocracy. In a meritocracy, rulers are not automatically considered the best rulers for life, but must demonstrate their abilities and achievements in order to maintain power. A plutocracy is a system of government led by the wealthy. There is often an overlap between the classification of a government as an aristocracy and a plutocracy, because wealth can enable individuals to portray their own qualities and merits as the best.

Commonwealth

A commonwealth is a state that is founded on law and that is united by a compact or by an agreement made by its citizens for the common good of the entire state and for the citizens of the state. In a commonwealth, supreme authority is held by the people. In the United States, the state of Kentucky, the state of Massachusetts, the state of Pennsylvania, and the state of Virginia are all classified as commonwealths. The term commonwealth is also used to describe Puerto Rico and the Northern Marianas Islands, which are both self-governing, autonomous political units that voluntarily associate themselves with the United States of America.

Federal Republic

A federal republic is a state that defines itself as both a federation and a republic. A federation is a state that is made up of multiple self-governing regions that are united by a central, federal government. The self-government of independent states is guaranteed by a constitution and is not able to be repealed by the central government. There are three countries that currently characterize themselves as federal republics. These three countries are the Federal Republic of Germany, the

Federal Republic of Nigeria, and the Federal Democratic Republic of Ethiopia.

Theocracy

A theocracy is a form of a government system in which religion or faith plays a significant role in the way that the government is run. Commonly, in countries that identify themselves as a theocracy, civil rulers are also the leaders of the dominant religion. In these countries, government policies are often strongly guided by religion. Usually, a theocratic government makes a claim to rule on behalf of God or another higher power. The administrative hierarchy of the government often serves as the administrative hierarchy of the dominant religion as well.

Socialist Republic

In a socialist republic, the constitution or other political doctrine stipulates that the republic operates under a socialist economic system, such as a Marxist system. Some socialist republics are under the power of a party whose platform is founded on communist ideology, and as such are referred to as communist states by Western nations. Examples of republics that use the term socialist in their names include the Democratic Socialist Republic of Sri Lanka and the former Socialist Federal Republic of Yugoslavia. Some countries that define themselves as socialist republics, such as India and Guyana, do so in their constitutions rather than in their names. Other countries that identify themselves as socialist republics include North Korea, the People's Republic of China, and Cuba.

Economic System

An economic system addresses the production, distribution and consumption of goods and services within society and focuses on solving the economic problems of the allocation and scarcity of resources. The composition of an economic system consists of people and institutions, and the relationships between them. The three questions that must be answered in an economic system are 1) what to produce, 2) how to produce it, and 3) for whom to produce. There are many different types of economic systems, which are often associated with particular ideologies and political systems. Examples of economic systems include market economies, mixed economies, planned economies, traditional economies, and participatory economies.

Tribalism

Tribalism was the first social system that humans created and coexisted in. It is a system in which society is divided into relatively independent groups referred to as tribes. In such a society, tribes themselves have some level of organizational structure, but there is generally very little organization between tribes. Tribes are typically characterized by simple internal organization and structure, with very few differences in social status between individuals. Some tribes nurture the belief that all individuals are equal, and many tribes do not embrace the concept of private property.

Feudalism

Feudalism is a political and economic system that was in existence in Europe from the ninth century through the fifteenth century. Feudalism in the Medieval Age was based on the relationships between lords and vassals and fiefs. A lord was a person who held a title of nobility and who owned land. A vassal was an individual who was loaned a piece of land by a lord. The piece of land that was owned by the lord and loaned to the vassal was referred to as a fief. In exchange for being loaned the fief, the vassal provided military service to the lord.

Capitalism

Capitalism is an economic system in which the means of production are privately owned, in which the investment of capital, and the production, distribution and prices of goods and services are determined in a free market, and in which the goal of production is to generate profits. The features of a capitalist economic system include a private sector, private property, free enterprise, and profit. Other features of a capitalist economic system include unequal distribution of wealth, competition, self-organization, the existence of markets, the existence of both a bourgeoisie class and a proletariat class, and the pursuit of self-interest.

Mixed Economy

A mixed economy is an economic system blending capitalism and socialism. Such a system is characterized by both private economic freedom and by centralized economic planning. The majority of Western countries, including the United States, have a mixed economy. Features of a mixed economy include the freedoms to possess means of production, to travel, to buy and sell, to hire and fire, to organize labor unions or associations, the freedom of communication, and the freedom to protest peacefully. In addition, mixed economies typically provide legal assistance, libraries, roads, schools, hospitals, protection of person and property both at home and abroad, subsidies to agriculture and other businesses, and government monopolies and government-granted monopolies, all of which are funded by taxes or subsidies. There are provisions for autonomy over personal finances, but mixed economies also include socially-oriented involuntary spending programs such as welfare, social security, and government subsidies for businesses. Mixed economies also impose environmental, labor, consumer, antitrust, intellectual property, corporate, and import and export laws, as well as taxes and fees.

Socialism

Socialism referrers to an economic system in which the means of production and the distribution of goods and services are owned collectively or are owned by a centralized government that often plans and controls the economy. In practice, socialism also refers to the economic phase in Marxist-Leninist theory that falls somewhere between capitalism and communism, in which collective ownership of the economy by the proletariat, or the working class, has not yet been achieved. The goal of a socialist economic system is to achieve collective ownership and, ultimately, to achieve a classless society.

Neo-Colonialism

Neocolonialism is a political and economic system in which a powerful country uses economic and political measures to extend, or to continue, its influence over less developed countries. The term was devised to describe circumstances at the international level after the fall of European colonial empires in the nineteenth and twentieth centuries, particularly the phenomenon of countries and multinational corporations seeking control over other countries through indirect means, such as economic policies, as opposed to the direct military-political control that traditional colonial powers sought. Many people argue that economic tools, such as restrictions on trade and embargos, that are employed by stronger,

more developed countries in their relations with less developed countries are reminiscent of colonial power.

Colonialism and Imperialism

Colonialism is a political and economic system that is defined as the extension of a nation's sovereignty over territory and people outside its own boundaries, often amounting to the exploitation of a weaker country by a relatively stronger country. Most often the stronger country is interested in the use of the weaker country's resources, including labor, to strengthen and enrich itself. Colonialism also refers to the set of beliefs and values that is used to validate and advance this system, particularly the belief that the culture and civilization of the relatively stronger colonizing country are superior to those of the relatively weaker colonized country. Imperialism is a policy of extending control or authority over foreign countries via territorial acquisition or by the establishment of economic and political control over other countries.

Nazism

Nazism was the ideology of the National Socialist German Workers Party which was led by Adolf Hitler in Nazi Germany from 1933 to 1945, during the Third Reich. Followers of Nazism believed that the Aryan race was superior to other races, and promoted Germanic racial supremacy and a strong, centrally governed state. Nazism is illegal in modern Germany, but small factions of Neo-Nazis continue to exist both in Germany and abroad. Nazis believed that military power would produce a strong nation, opposed multilingualism and multiculturalism, and sought the unification of all German-speaking individuals. Qualities of Nazism included racism, anti-Semitism, the desire for the

- 63 -

creation of a master race, anti-Slavism, the belief in the superiority of the White, Germanic, Aryan or Nordic races, anti-Marxism, anti-Communism, and anti-Bolshevism, rejection of democracy, social Darwinism, eugenics, environmental protection, rejection of the modern art movement and an embrace of classical art, and defense of the Nazi flag.

Command/Planned Economy

A planned economy is an economic system in which decisions about the production, allocation and consumption of goods and services is planned in advance; planning can be carried out in either a centralized or decentralized approach. In most planned economies, the plans are carried out by means of commands; therefore planned economies are also commonly referred to as command economies. An economic system that is centrally-planned by a government is generally referred to as economic statism. Economic statism, by definition, is the practice of giving a centralized government control over economic planning and policy.

Libertarianism

Libertarianism is an ideology that seeks to maximize individual rights, private property rights, and free market capitalism. Individuals who subscribe to the ideology of libertarianism believe that people should have the freedom to do what they will with their bodies and their private property as long as they do not coerce others to do the same. They also believe that individuals should have the liberty to make their own moral choices as long as they do not use coercion to prevent others from exercising the same liberty, and that government should not prevent an individual from making a moral choice or impose moral obligations on people. Libertarians advocate

minimum government involvement except to protect liberty and prevent coercion. In addition, libertarians support capitalism and oppose social welfare, and also oppose government spending and programming that are not aimed at protecting liberty.

Liberalism

Liberalism is an ideology based on the autonomy of individuals. Liberalism favors civil and political liberties, and seeks to maximize those liberties under law and ensure protection from arbitrary authority. A system characterized by liberalism would possess a pluralistic liberal democratic system of government, a rule of law, the free exchange of ideas, and economic competition. The basic principles of liberalism include transparency, individual and civil rights, particularly the right to life, liberty, and property, equal rights for all citizens under law, and government by the consent of the governed, which is guaranteed through elections. Liberalism also favors laissez-faire economics, the free market, and the gold standard.

Nationalism

Nationalism is an ideology based upon the ideal that identification with a nation, ethnicity or nationality is an essential and defining part of human social existence. Nationalism is thus a universal ideology. However, nationalism also refers to the ideology that one national identity is superior to others, and to the view that nations benefit from acting independently rather than collectively. This view of nationalism often spawns nationalist movements, which make political claims on behalf of particular nations. Nationalists differentiate between nations based on specific criteria, and also differentiate between individual people based on which nation they are a member of. The criteria used to define national identity include ethnicity, a common language, a common culture, and common values. Nationalism has had an extremely significant impact on world history and geopolitics since the nation-state has become the prevailing form of state. Most people in the world currently live in states which are nation-states.

American Liberalism

American liberalism is a political ideology which is derived from classical liberalism. Like classical liberalism, American liberalism is defined by the ideal of individual liberty. However, American liberalism typically rejects laissez faire economics and instead advocates for the creation and maintenance of institutions that foster social and economic equity. American liberalism began in the beginning of the twentieth century, and started to decline in the 1970s. American liberalism features support for government social programs, increased funding for public education, labor unions, regulation of business, civil rights, voting rights, reproductive rights, strong environmental regulations, public transportation, minimum wage requirements, government funding to alternative energy research, animal rights, gun control, and a progressive tax system. People who subscribe to American liberalism oppose the death penalty.

Green Politics

Green politics is a political ideology based on environmentalism and sustainability. It is seen as an alternative to both left and right-wing views, and individuals identifying themselves with the left or right tend to view green politics as distinct from their own ideology. As a movement, green politics typically grows at a slow rate but does not readily lose

support to other views or parties over time. Some of the features of green politics include support of consensus decision making, participatory democracy and deliberative democracy; green taxes; alternative measures of economic growth; opposition to the subsidy of pollution by government; opposition to nuclear power, persistent organic pollutants, and biological forms of pollution; investing in human capital; accounting reform; an end to the War on Drugs in the United States and Europe; an end to the War on Terrorism and the curtailment of civil rights.

Conservatism

Conservatism is a political ideology that is founded on traditional values, a distrust of government and resistance to changes in the established social order. Most conservative political parties are right-wing, but some countries do have conservative political parties that are left-wing. All conservatives place a high value on tradition, which refers to standards and institutions that have been demonstrated to foster good. Conservatives view traditional values as authoritative, and judge the world by the standards they have come to believe in, including a belief in God. Conservatives consider tradition to be above the political process. They also disagree with the laws and constitutions of liberal democracies that allow behavior that is in opposition to traditional values. Conservatives in a democracy opt to participate, separate, or resist. Participation on the part of conservatives in a democracy usually takes the form of liberal republican politics, in which conservatives use government policy to promote their values. The imposition of conservative values on the public is typical of nationalist or religious conservatives.

Republicanism

Republicanism is a political ideology founded on the concept of a nation being governed by an elected representative rather than a monarch. Today, the elected representative is most often referred to as the President. A republic is a state in which sovereignty resides with the people, as well as a political system in which individual liberty is protected through the power of citizens to elect representatives. These representatives are responsible to the citizens who elected them and govern according to law. Republicanism also represents the ideologies of the political parties that identify themselves as the Republican Party.

Pacifism

Pacifism is an ideology that is based on opposition to war. Pacifism varies from a preference for the use of non-military means in resolving disputes to complete opposition to the use of violence or force in any situation. Pacifism may be based on principle or pragmatism. Pacifism based on principle is founded on the belief that war, violence, force and coercion are morally wrong. Pacifism based on pragmatism is founded on the belief that there are preferable means of resolving disputes than war, and that the costs of war outweigh the benefits. An individual who opposes war is often referred to as a dove or dovish, alluding to the peaceful nature of the dove.

Feminism

Feminism is an ideology founded on the belief that there should be social, political and economic equality between the sexes. This belief has manifested itself in a social movement known as the feminist movement, which advocates equal rights for women. As such, feminism typically focuses on issues that pertain to women, such as reproductive rights, domestic violence, maternity leave, equal pay, sexual harassment, sexual discrimination, and sexual violence, as well as on the themes of patriarchy, stereotyping, objectification, and oppression. In the 1960s and 70s, feminism focused on issues faced by Western, white, middle-class women while claiming to represent all women. Feminism has since progressed to focus on the connection between gender and sexuality with other social factors, such as race and class. Modern feminism addresses issues that cross class, racial, cultural, and religious boundaries, as well as issues that are specific and pertinent to individual cultures. Feminism also addresses whether particular issues associated with women, such as rape, incest, and mothering, are universal issues.

Public Policy

Public policy is the study of how the various levels of government formulate and implement policies. Public policy also refers to the set of policies that a government adopts and implements, including laws, plans, actions, and behaviors, for the purpose of governing society. Public policy is developed and adapted through the process of policy analysis. Public policy analysis is the systematic evaluation of alternative means of reaching social goals. Public policy is divided into various policy areas, including domestic policy, foreign policy, healthcare policy, education policy, criminal policy, national defense policy, and energy policy.

Police State

A police state is a form of a totalitarian political system. A nation does not identify itself as a police state; rather, the characterization is applied by critics of the nation. A police state is regulated by police, who exercise power on behalf of an executive authority. It is very difficult to challenge the police and question their conduct in a police state, and there is no rule of law; the law is simply the will of the leader. The police state is based on the concept of enlightened despotism, under which the leader exercises absolute power with the goal of providing for the good of a nation; opposition to government policy is an offense against authority, and therefore against the nation itself.

Because public dissent is not allowed, people who oppose the government must do so in secret. Therefore, the police must resort to the use of informers and secret police to seek out dissenters.

Domestic PolicyForeign Policy

Domestic policy entails all government policy decisions, laws, programs, plans, actions and behaviors that address internal state matters. Examples of domestic policy include tax policy, social security and welfare programs, environmental laws and regulations, and regulations on businesses and their practices. In contrast, foreign policy addresses how a country will engage with other countries. Foreign policy is typically created with the intention of protecting and promoting a country's national interests, national security, ideological goals, and economic prosperity. Foreign policy can be directed towards peaceful cooperation with other countries, as well as towards aggression, war, or exploitation. The creation of foreign policy is typically the responsibility of a country's head of government and foreign minister. In the U.S., the legislature also has substantial power and influence, which is reflected in the authority of Congress to pass Foreign Relations Authorization bills.

Paradigms and Morphosyntax

The concept of a paradigm is closely related to inflection. The paradigm of a lexeme is the set of all of its word forms and is organized by their grammatical categories. Examples of paradigms include verb conjugation or declensions of nouns. Word forms of lexemes can normally be arranged into tables and classified by shared features that include tense, aspect, number, case, gender, or mood. Categories that are used to group word forms into paradigms cannot be chosen arbitrarily and must be categorized with regard to syntactic rules. The main difference between word formation and inflection is that inflectional forms are organized into paradigms which are defined by requirements of syntactic rules. The area of morphology dealing with that relationship is called morphosyntax and is related to inflection and paradigms, but not compounding or word formation.

Practice test

Practice questions

1. Thomas Paine's Common Sense influenced which American document that ultimately helped shape the Constitution?
   - a. The Articles of Confederation
   - b. The Declaration of Independence
   - c. Bill of Rights
   - d. The Treaty of Greenville

2. One reason the Articles of Confederation created a weak government was because it limited Congress's ability to do what?
   - a. Declare war
   - b. Conduct a census
   - c. Vote
   - d. Tax

3. The philosophy of the late 17th-18th centuries that influenced the Constitution was from the Age of:
   - a. Enlightenment
   - b. Empire
   - c. Discovery
   - d. Industry

4. The votes of how many states were needed to ratify the Constitution?
   - a. Five
   - b. Ten
   - c. Nine
   - d. Seven

5. Virginian _____ advocated a stronger central government and was influential at the Constitutional Convention.
   - a. Benjamin Franklin
   - b. James Madison
   - c. George Mason
   - d. Robert Yates

6. Power divided between local and central branches of government is a definition of what term?
   - a. Bicameralism
   - b. Checks and balances
   - c. Legislative oversight
   - d. Federalism

7. The Senate and the House of Representatives are an example of:
   a. Bicameralism
   b. Checks and balances
   c. Legislative oversight
   d. Federalism

8. The civil rights act that outlawed segregation in schools and public places also:
   a. Gave minorities the right to vote
   b. Established women's right to vote
   c. Outlawed unequal voter registration
   d. Provided protection for children

9. Which court case established the Court's ability to overturn laws that violated the Constitution?
   a. Miranda v. Arizona
   b. Marbury v. Madison
   c. United States v. Curtiss-Wright Export Corporation
   d. Brown v. Board of Education of Topeka

10. The first ten amendments to the Constitution are more commonly known as:
   a. The Civil Rights Act
   b. Common law
   c. The Equal Protection clause
   d. The Bill of Rights

11. How many Southern states originally ratified the 14th Amendment?
   a. Three
   b. Five
   c. One
   d. Ten

12. When the Senate held an impeachment hearing against Andrew Johnson for overstepping his authority, what did they invoke?
   a. Checks and balances
   b. Bicameralism
   c. Legislative oversight
   d. Supremacy

13. Which Supreme Court case enforced the civil rights of citizens to not incriminate themselves?
   a. Marbury v. Madison
   b. Miranda v. Arizona
   c. Youngstown Sheet and Tube Company v. Sawyer
   d. United States v. Carolene Products Company

14. What judicial system did America borrow from England?
  a. Due process
  b. Federal law
  c.Commerce law
  d. Common law

15. The writers of The Federalist Papers published under the pen name "Publius." Who were the authors?
  a. James Madison, John Jay, and Alexander Hamilton
  b. George Washington, Thomas Jefferson, and James Madison
  c. Alexander Hamilton, Benjamin Franklin, and Thomas Jefferson
  d. Benjamin Franklin, John Jay, and Thomas Jefferson

16. To be President of the United States, one must meet these three requirements:
  a. The President must be college educated, at least 30 years old, and a natural citizen
  b. The President must be a natural citizen, have lived in the U.S. for 14 years, and have a college education
  c. The President must be a natural citizen, be at least 35 years old, and have lived in the U.S. for 14 years
  d. The President must be at least 30 years old, be a natural citizen, and have lived in the U.S. for 14 years

17. The President may serve a maximum of _____ according to the ___ Amendment.
  a. Three four-year terms; 23rd
  b. Two four-year terms; 22nd
  c. One four-year term; 22nd
  d. Three four-year terms; 23rd

18. How many Commissioners does the President appoint to the SEC?
  a. Five
  b. One
  c. Two
  d. Ten

19. The Office of Management and Budget helps the President prepare the federal budget. What are they part of?
  a. United States Trade Representative
  b. Federal Reserve Board
  c. Securities and Exchange Commission
  d. Executive Office of the President

20. The Vice President succeeds the President in case of death, illness or impeachment. What is the order of succession for the next three successors, according to the Presidential Succession Act of 1947?
  a. President Pro Tempore of the Senate, Secretary of State, and Secretary of Defense
  b. Speaker of the House, President Pro Tempore of the Senate, and Secretary of State
  c. President Pro Tempore of the Senate, Speaker of the House, and Secretary of State
  d. Secretary of State, Secretary of Defense, and Speaker of the House

21. The President has the power to veto legislation. How is this power limited?
    I. Congress can override the veto
    II. The President cannot line veto
    III. The President cannot propose legislation
    a. I and III
    b. II only
    c. I and II
    d. I only

22. The President serves as Commander-in-Chief. What are the President's two limitations in that role?
    a. The President cannot declare war or oversee military regulations
    b. The President cannot enforce blockades or declare war
    c. The President cannot enforce quarantines or oversee military regulations
    d. The President cannot enforce blockades or quarantines

23. What are the official requirements for serving in the House of Representatives?
    a. A member of the House must be at least 30 years old, a U.S. citizen for a minimum of nine years, and a resident of the state and district he represents
    b. A member of the House must be at least 25 years old, a natural citizen, and a resident of the state he represents
    c. A member of the House must be at least 30 years old, a natural citizen, and a resident of the state and district he represents
    d. A member of the House must be at least 25 years old, a U.S. citizen for a minimum of seven years, and a resident of the state he represents

24. What are the official requirements for becoming a Senator?
    a. A Senator must be at least 35 years old, a U.S. citizen for a minimum of seven years, and a resident of the state he represents
    b. A Senator must be at least 30 years old, a U.S. citizen for a minimum of nine years, and a resident of the state he represents
    c. A Senator must be at least 25 years old, a U.S. citizen for a minimum of nine years, and a resident of the state and district he represents
    d. A Senator must be at least 30 years old, a natural citizen, and a resident of the state he represents

25. Senators were once chosen by state legislatures. When were they first elected by popular vote?
    a. 1912
    b. 1917
    c. 1913
    d. 1915

26. Who may write a bill?
    a. Anyone
    b. A member of the House
    c. A Senator
    d. Any member of Congress

27. Congressional elections are held every _____ years.
    a. Four
    b. Two
    c. Six
    d. Three

28. How is a tie broken in the Senate?
    a. The President Pro Tempore casts the deciding vote
    b. The Speaker of the House votes
    c. They vote again
    d. The Vice President votes

29. A newly introduced bill is first given to a _____ where it is either accepted, amended or rejected completely.
    a. Full committee
    b. Conference committee
    c. Subcommittee
    d. Senate committee

30. The House Committee on Oversight and Government Reform oversees and reforms government operations. Which Senate committee works with that committee?
    a. Senate Committee on Banking, Housing, and Urban Affairs
    b. Senate Committee on Homeland Security and Government Affairs
    c. Senate Committee on Rules and Administration
    d. Senate Appropriations Committee

31. How are members of the Federal Judiciary chosen?
    a. They are elected by voters
    b. They are appointed by the President and confirmed by the House of Representatives
    c. They are chosen by a committee
    d. They are appointed by the President and confirmed by the Senate

32. How long can members of the Federal Judiciary serve?
    a. Four years
    b. Eight years
    c. For life
    d. Six years

33. Article III judges who can retire but still try cases on a full-time or part-time basis are called _____.
    a. Recalled judges
    b. Senior judges
    c. Chief judges
    d. Elder judges

34. How many judges are on a panel that decides federal appeals?
   a. Five
   b. Three
   c. Nine
   d. Six

35. What petition needs to be filed to request that the Supreme Court hear a case?
   a. Writ of certiorari
   b. Writ of habeas corpus
   c. Writ of mandamus
   d. Writ of attachment

36. Most federal judges have served as local judges, lawyers, and law professors. These are
_____ qualifications.
   a. Formal
   b. Required
   c. Informal
   d. Recommended

37. The Supreme Court has nine members. How is this number determined?
   a. It is outlined in the Constitution
   b. Congress determines the number
   c. The President determines the number
   d. The Court decides on the number

38. Criminal cases are tried under:
       I. State law
       II. Federal law
       III. Civil court
   a. I and III
   b. II only
   c. I only
   d. I and II

39. The executive, legislative, and judicial branches of government compose:
   a. The federal government
   b. The state government
   c. Both A and B
   d. None of the above

40. Most state governments have a bicameral legislature. Which one of the following states
does not?
   a. Utah
   b. Nebraska
   c. Washington
   d. Louisiana

41. What does the 10th Amendment establish?
   a. Any power not given to the federal government belongs to the state and the people
   b. The President is responsible for executing and enforcing laws created by Congress
   c. Congress has the authority to declare war
   d. The Supreme Court has the authority to interpret the Constitution

42. Parks and recreation services, police and fire departments, housing services, emergency medical services, municipal courts, transportation services, and public works usually fall under the jurisdiction of which body of government?
   a. State government
   b. Federal government
   c. Federal agencies
   d. Local government

43. How is the jurisdiction of federal courts usually decided?
   a. By the President
   b. By Congress
   c. By the voters
   d. By the Supreme Court

44. How must inferior courts interpret the law?
   a. According to the Supreme Court's interpretation
   b. According to the Constitution
   c. However they choose
   d. According to the political climate

45. How was the Vice President chosen before the 12th Amendment was ratified?
   a. The President chose the Vice President
   b. Congress chose the Vice President
   c. The Vice President came in second in the Electoral College
   d. There was no Vice President

46. What portion of the federal budget is dedicated to transportation, education, national resources, the environment, and international affairs?
   a. Mandatory spending
   b. Discretionary spending
   c. Undistributed offsetting receipts
   d. Official budget outlays

47. The primary expense for most state and local governments is:
   a. Emergency medical services
   b. Transportation services
   c. Police and fire departments
   d. Education

48. Which court has jurisdiction in bankruptcy cases?
    a. State courts
    b. Municipal courts
    c. Federal courts
    d. The Supreme Court

49. Every citizen 18 years of age and older has the constitutional right to vote. What do states govern in the voting process?
    a. The registration for elections
    b. The administration of elections
    c. Both A and B
    d. State governments are not involved in federal elections

50. Which statement describes the authority of most local officials?
    a. Members of local government are generally elected by the people, but their authority is granted by the state
    b. Members of local government are given their authority directly from the people
    c. Members of local government have constitutionally-granted authority
    d. Members of local government are elected by the people, but the state Supreme Court determines their authority

51. Which branch of the government employs the Armed Forces?
    a. The judicial branch
    b. The legislative branch
    c. State governments
    d. The executive branch

52. The Animal and Plant Health Inspection Service, the Food and Nutrition Service, and the Forest Service are members of which department?
    a. The Department of Health and Human Services
    b. The Department of Agriculture
    c. The Department of the Interior
    d. The Department of Transportation

53. A filibuster is used to delay a bill. Where can a filibuster take place?
        I. The House
        II. The Senate
        III. Committees
    a. I only
    b. II only
    c. I and II
    d. I, II, and III

54. Which organization is maintained by Congress to oversee the effectiveness of government spending?
    a. The House Committee on Oversight and Government Reform
    b. The Office of Management and Budget
    c. Government Accountability Office
    d. The Department of the Interior

55. Disagreements between individuals or organizations are tried in:
    a. Civil court
    b. Criminal court
    c. Federal court
    d. State court

56. What best describes the way Washington, D.C. is governed?
    a. Congress has ultimate authority
    b. Washington, D.C. has a local government similar to that of other cities in the area
    c. There is no local government in place
    d. There is a mayor and city council, but Congress has the authority to overrule their decisions

57. The Political Affairs Agency is part of which department?
    a. The Department of State
    b. The Department of Defense
    c. The Department of Homeland Security
    d. The Department of Security

58. How many Vice Presidents have succeeded as President?
    a. Four
    b. Thirteen
    c. Nine
    d. Five

59. All of the Cabinet members have the title Secretary except for which member?
    a. The head of the Department of Agriculture
    b. The head of the Department of Justice
    c. The head of the Department of Commerce
    d. The head of the Department of Defense

60. What percentage of votes does the Senate need to pass a bill?
    a. Two-thirds majority
    b. A simple majority
    c. A supermajority
    d. Three-quarters majority

61. Which states do NOT generate income by implementing a sales tax?
    a. Alaska, Texas, Vermont, and New Hampshire
    b. Delaware, Oregon, Texas, Louisiana, and Montana
    c. New Hampshire, Oregon, Louisiana, Delaware, and Vermont
    d. Alaska, Delaware, Montana, New Hampshire, and Oregon

62. Who negotiates treaties?
    a. The President
    b. The House of Representatives
    c. Ambassadors
    d. The Senate

63. There are 435 members in the House of Representatives. How many CANNOT vote?
    a. Four
    b. Two
    c. Six
    d. None of the above

64. Which branch(es) of the federal government issue(s) subpoenas?
        I. The executive branch
        II. The legislative branch
        III. The judicial branch
    a. III only
    b. I and III
    c. II and III
    d. II only

65. Who is responsible for ensuring food safety?
        I. Federal agencies
        II. State agencies
        III. Local agencies
    a. I only
    b. II and III
    c. I and II
    d. I, II, and III

66. What is the role of the Chief Justice, according to Article I?
    a. The Chief Justice heads the Supreme Court
    b. The Chief Justice heads trials involving the President
    c. The President appoints the Chief Justice
    d. The Chief Justice is one of nine Supreme Court judges

67. Which statement is true of an appellate court?
    a. The appellate court simply reviews the previous case and does not use new testimony or evidence
    b. The appellate court is a new jury trial
    c. The appellate court requires new evidence and testimony
    d. The appellate court's decision is always final

68. What does the term "en banc" mean?
    a. A document requesting an appeal
    b. A petition to the Supreme Court
    c. A larger group of judges who review an appellate court's decision
    d. The legal argument of an appellant

69. Which agency is not part of the Cabinet?
    a. U.S. Department of Agriculture
    b. Environmental Protection Agency
    c. Department of Commerce
    d. Department of Energy

70. Which is true of the President's authority?
    a. The President has the authority to declare war
    b. The President has the authority to grant pardons and clemencies for federal crimes, except in cases of impeachment
    c. The President can serve three terms
    d. The President has the authority to appoint the Speaker of the House

71. What would be considered an informal qualification for being elected President?
    a. The President must be well-traveled
    b. The President must be at least 40 years old
    c. The President must have good character
    d. The President must be a natural citizen

72. How is a tie in the Electoral College broken to choose the President?
    a. Each state's delegation in the House of Representatives gets a vote, and the majority wins
    b. Each state's delegation in the Senate gets a vote, and the majority wins
    c. The former Vice President becomes President
    d. The Speaker of the House casts the deciding vote

73. Which of the following statements about the House is true?
    a. The House does not approve appointments or ratify treaties
    b. Every member of the House of Representatives is given one vote
    c. The members of the House are elected every three years
    d. The House must approve appointments of the Vice Presidency and any treaty involving foreign trade

74. Which constitutional requirement for passing a bill rarely happens?
    a. The leader of the majority party decides when to place the bill on the calendar for consideration before Congress
    b. The versions of a bill that pass through both houses of Congress and are signed by the President must have the exact same wording
    c. The number and kind of amendments introduced in the House are limited
    d. A filibuster needs a supermajority vote to be broken

75. How many members of the Electoral College represent Washington, D.C.?
    a. One
    b. Two
    c. Three
    d. Five

76. How are federal judges removed from office?
    a. They are impeached in the House and convicted in the Senate
    b. They are impeached and convicted in the Senate
    c. They are convicted in the House and impeached in the Senate
    d. They are impeached in the House

77. Cases involving diplomats and ambassadors fall under the jurisdiction of which court?
    a. District courts
    b. State courts
    c. Supreme Court
    d. Federal Court of Appeals

78. What does NOT help ensure a two-party system?
    a. A winner-take-all system
    b. A representative system
    c. State and federal laws
    d. Political culture

79. What effect do minor political parties have on the elections?
    a. They are too small to threaten major parties
    b. They take funding away from major parties
    c. They often work with the major parties
    d. They can potentially take votes away from major parties

80. Which of the following statements about special interest groups is true?
    a. Special interest groups do not utilize mass media
    b. Business groups favor Republican candidates
    c. A few million supporters concentrated in a few states will have more influence than the same number of supporters spread throughout the nation

    d. Special interest groups file amicus curiae briefs in cases in which they are not directly involved

81. Delegates awarded to Puerto Rico, Guam, and American Samoa in the Democratic National Convention are:
    a. PLEO delegates
    b. Base delegates
    c. District delegates
    d. Bonus delegates

82. What is the main difference between a primary election and a caucus?
    a. A primary election is privately run by political parties, and a caucus is held by local governments
    b. Caucuses are always held on the same day, but the dates of state primaries vary
    c. A caucus is privately run by political parties, and a primary is an indirect election run by state and local governments
    d. Primary elections are all held on the same date, but the dates of caucuses vary

83. What are campaign funds given directly to a candidate called?
    a. Soft money
    b. Hard money
    c. Bundling
    d. Independent expenditure

84. Presidential candidates are eligible for public funding if they raise $5,000 per state in how many states?
    a. Twenty
    b. Ten
    c. Twenty-five
    d. Seventeen

85. What is a committee that raises money for political candidates and is formed by business, labor, or other special interest groups?
    a. Party
    b. Lobby
    c. PLEO
    d. PAC

86. What effect do grassroots organizations NOT have on elections?
    a. They raise money for campaigns
    b. They register voters and recruit volunteers
    c. They completely align with party platforms
    d. They educate voters and communicate directly to local citizens

87. What are common social demographics for liberals?
    a. Single, religious, and educated
    b. Single, secular, and educated
    c. Married, religious, and educated
    d. Married, secular, and gun owners

88. People are typically made aware of political, facts, and values through family, friends, society, and:
    a. Media
    b. Census takers
    c. History
    d. Gun ownership

89. What does survey sampling help measure?
    a. Political values
    b. Political socialization
    c. Public opinion
    d. Private opinion

90. What demographics have recently shown support for Democratic candidates?
    a. Men and young voters
    b. Women and young voters
    c. Women and gun owners
    d. Men and gun owners

91. What is the term for the general agreement on fundamental principles of governance and the values supporting them?
    a. Rule of law
    b. Nationalism
    c. Political culture
    d. Democratic consensus

92. How do the media and public opinion or polls influence one another?
    a. The media does not affect polls or public opinion
    b. The media is unbiased and simply presents candidates
    c. The way the media presents a candidate can determine polls and the polls influence media portrayal
    d. The media does not reflect polls

93. What do the American labor union movement, the antislavery movement, the women's suffrage movement, and the civil rights movement have in common?
    a. They all used political protest
    b. They all appealed to legal precedent
    c. They all came from political homogeneity
    d. They were all protected by the commerce clause

94. What method is NOT used to create a poll?
    a. Internet sites
    b. Phone interviews
    c. Observation
    d. Face to face interviews

95. If a party carries a state in a Presidential election, who are named as electors in the Electoral College?
    a. Political machines
    b. Party activists
    c. Executive officials
    d. Party workers

96. What type of representation is based on the number of votes each party receives?
    a. Coalition
    b. Single member districts
    c. The Electoral College
    d. Proportional representation

97. Which influences are stronger in adult political thinking?
    a. Family, media, and class
    b. Peers, news, and media
    c. Class, peers, and media
    d. Family, peers, and news

98. Gun control, strong environmental laws, social programs, and opposition to the death penalty are what kind of issues?
    a. Compassion issues
    b. Activism
    c. Regional issues
    d. Religious issues

99. What group petitions the government?
    a. Common Cause
    b. Party leaders
    c. Lobbyists
    d. Party activists

100. Political affiliation is an example of what?
    a. Personal opinion
    b. Schema
    c. Public opinion
    d. Personal interest

101. How did the attacks of 2001 influence American nationalism?
    I. Negatively
    II. Positively
    III. Not at all
    a. I and II
    b. I only
    c. III only
    d. II only

102. The constitutional rights of citizens are protected in what?
    a. Bicameral legislature
    b. Authoritarian regimes
    c. Constitutional republics
    d. Pure democracies

103. Socialists believe that equality requires:
    a. No private property
    b. Government influence
    c. A free market
    d. A mixed system

104. Which supranational institution regulates international trade, human rights, and nation development?
    a. The UN
    b. The EEOC
    c. The UNDP
    d. The GOP

105. The media is closely monitored under:
   a. The democratic system
   b. The Presidential system
   c. The authoritarian system
   d. The Parliamentary system

106. What was an early difference between Marxism and fascism?
   a. Fascism came out of socialism and Marxism from capitalism
   b. Fascists were nationalists and Marxists had an international focus
   c. Fascists wanted to defeat capitalism and Marxists wanted to preserve private property
   d. Marxism originally wanted to preserve class structure and fascism supported capitalism

107. Public policy is developed at what level?
   a. State level
   b. Local level
   c. Federal level
   d. All of the above

108. What are the three stages of the public policy making process?
   a. Problems, players, and the policy
   b. Religious leaders, cultural institutions, and the private sector
   c. Agenda-setting, option-formulation, and implementation
   d. Law, decisions, and actions

109. Modern separation of powers preserves which principle?
   a. Mixed government
   b. Democracy
   c. Parliamentary system
   d. Presidential system

110. The Head of State and Chief Executive are two separate offices in which system?
   a. Presidential system
   b. Authoritarian system
   c. Parliamentary system
   d. Representative democracy

111. What is a similarity between the Presidential system of the U.S. and the Parliamentary system of Great Britain?
   a. Both the President and Prime Minister serve as Head of State
   b. Both the President and Prime Minister can be removed from office
   c. Both the President and Prime Minister are chosen by the legislature
   d. Both the President and Prime Minister are elected directly by the people

112. Which system of government formally nationalizes the private sector?
    a. Capitalism
    b. Corporatism
    c. Nationalism
    d. Socialism

113. What is the result of a free market combined with government regulation?
    a. Mixed economy
    b. Corporatism
    c. Socialism
    d. Nationalism

114. What institution affiliated with the UN is responsible for stabilizing foreign exchange rates?
    a. UNDP
    b. IMF
    c. EEOC
    d. PLEO

115. Direct democracy is used more often on which level?
    a. National
    b. State
    c. Local
    d. Supranational

116. Special interest groups are considered experts in certain public policy:
    a. Definitions
    b. Processes
    c. Implementation
    d. Areas

117. Authoritarian regimes often have which type of legislature?
    a. Bicameral
    b. Unicameral
    c. Multi-cameral
    d. Representative

118. What does nationalism accomplish?
    a. Nationalism legitimizes authority and establishes unity
    b. Nationalism creates chaos
    c. Nationalism causes division
    d. Nationalism causes people to question their leaders

119. What kind of nation is made up of special interest groups focused on the civil liberties influencing public policy?
    a. Fascist
    b. Communist
    c. Pluralist
    d. Socialist

120. What do Marxists and capitalists have in common?
   a. They both believe in privatizing land ownership
   b. They both support free international trade
   c. They both support nationalization of the private sector
   d. They both support special interest groups

Answers and explanations

1. B: Published in early 1776, Common Sense condemned hereditary kingship. The pamphlet was popular in Colonial America, and even George Washington noticed its effect on the general population. Later that same year, Jefferson drafted the Declaration of Independence.

2. D: Congress did not have the authority to levy taxes under the Articles of Confederation. Without the ability to levy taxes, there was no way to finance programs, which weakened the government.

3. A: The Age of Enlightenment was a time of scientific and philosophical achievement. Also called the Age of Reason, human thought and reason were prized.

4. C: The Constitution was not ratified immediately. Only five states accepted it in early 1788; Massachusetts, New York, Rhode Island, and Virginia were originally opposed to the Constitution. Rhode Island reluctantly accepted it in 1790.

5. B: James Madison was a close friend of Thomas Jefferson and supported a stronger central government. George Mason and Robert Yates were both against expanding federal authority over the states. Benjamin Franklin was a proponent of a strong federal government, but he was from Massachusetts.

6. D: Federalists who helped frame the Constitution believed the central government needed to be stronger than what was established under the Articles of Confederation. Anti-federalists were against this and feared a strong federal government. A system of checks and balances was established to prevent the central government from taking too much power.

7. A: The Senate and House of Representatives make up a bicameral legislature. The Great Compromise awarded seats in the Senate equally to each state, while the seats in the House of Representatives were based on population.

8. C: The Civil Rights Act of 1964 affected the Jim Crowe laws in the Southern states. Many minorities suffered under unfair voting laws and segregation. President Lyndon Johnson signed the Civil Rights Act of 1964 into law after the 1963 assassination of President Kennedy, who championed the reform.

9. B: President John Adams appointed William Marbury as Justice of the Peace, but Secretary of State James Madison never delivered the commission. Marbury claimed that under the Judiciary Act of 1789, the Supreme Court could order his commission be given to him. The Supreme Court denied Marbury's petition citing that the Judiciary Act of 1789 was unconstitutional, although they believed he was entitled to his commission.

10. D: The Bill of Rights was drafted by Congress to limit the authority of the government and protect the rights of individual citizens from abuse by the federal government. It was the first document to detail the rights of private citizens.

11. C: Tennessee was the only Southern state to ratify the 14th Amendment. Although Southern states that ratified this amendment could be readmitted to the Union with more reform, President Andrew Johnson, who was at odds with Congress, advised them against it.

12. A: Checks and balances were established to keep one branch of government from taking too much authority. When Johnson violated the Tenure of Office Act by replacing Secretary of War Edwin Stanton, Johnson was impeached, but the final vote in the Senate trial came up one vote short of the number needed to convict him.

13. B: The Supreme Court ruled that statements made in interrogation are not admissible unless the defendant is informed of the right to an attorney and waives that right. The case of Miranda v. Arizona was consolidated with Westover v. United States, Vignera v. New York, and California v. Stewart.

14. D: America is a common law country because English common law was adopted in all states except Louisiana. Common law is based on precedent, and changes over time. Each state develops its own common laws.

15. A: James Madison, John Jay, and Alexander Hamilton published The Federalist in the Independent Journal in New York. It was a response to the Anti-Federalists in New York, who were slow to ratify the Constitution because they feared it gave the central government too much authority.

16. C: The President must be a natural citizen, be at least 35 years old, and have lived in the U.S. for 14 years. There is no education requirement for becoming President. Truman did not have a college education, but most Presidents have degrees.

17. B: Most Presidents have only served two terms, a precedent established by George Washington. Ulysses S. Grant and Theodore Roosevelt sought third terms; however, only Franklin D. Roosevelt served more than two terms. He served a third term and won a fourth, but died in its first year. The 22nd Amendment was passed by Congress in 1947 and ratified in 1951. It officially limited the President to two terms, and a Vice President who serves two years as President only can be elected for one term.

18. A: The Securities Exchange Act of 1934 established the Securities and Exchange Commission, which has five commissioners (one for each division) who serve staggered five-year terms. They are appointed by the President, who also chooses the Chairman of the Commission. No more than three of the commissioners can be in the same party to prevent partisanship.

19. D: The Office of Management and Budget is part of the Executive Office of the President (EOP). The EOP is a group of Presidential advisers and has been in place since Theodore Roosevelt. The President appoints members directly, but some positions like the Director of the Office of Management and Budget need Senate approval.

20. B: The Presidential Succession Act lists the Speaker of the House, President Pro Tempore of the Senate, and Secretary of State next in succession after the Vice President. However, anyone who succeeds as President must meet all of the legal qualifications.

21. C: The President has the power to veto legislation directly or use a pocket veto by not signing a bill within ten days after receiving it. Congress adjourns during this time period. A veto can be overridden if two-thirds of the House and the two-thirds of the Senate both agree. The President must veto a complete bill and does not have the authority to veto sections or lines.

22. A: The President of the United States serves as Commander-in-Chief, but the writers of the Constitution, who feared how authority was used by monarchs, limited the President's power in this role. The President cannot declare war or oversee military regulations, although Presidents have traditionally authorized the use of force without war being declared.

23. D: A member of the House must be at least 25 years old, a U.S. citizen for a minimum of seven years, and a resident of the state he represents. Members of the House do not necessarily need to reside in the districts they represent.

24. B: A Senator must be at least 30 years old, a U.S. citizen for a minimum of nine years, and a resident of the state he represents. Every state elects two Senators, and individual districts are represented in the House of Representatives.

25. C: The 17th Amendment was ratified in 1913. This amendment allowed the citizens to choose their Senators by holding elections and participating in a popular vote.

26. A: Anyone may write a bill, but only a member of Congress can introduce a bill. The President often suggests bills. Bills can change drastically throughout the review process.

27. B: Members of the House are elected for two-year terms. Senators serve six-year terms, but the elections are staggered so roughly one-third of the Senate is elected every two years.

28. D: The Vice President also serves as the President of the Senate. If a tie occurs in the Senate, the Vice President casts his vote to break the tie.

29. C: A bill is usually first reviewed by the appropriate subcommittee. The subcommittee can accept the bill, amend the bill, or reject the bill. If the subcommittee accepts or amends the bill, they send it to the full committee for review. Expert witnesses and testimony are all part of committee review.

30. The correct answer is B. The Senate Committee on Homeland Security and Government Affairs is a standing committee that oversees and reforms government operations and exercises the congressional power of government oversight.

31. D: According to Article III of the Constitution, Justices of the Supreme Court, judges of the courts of appeals and district courts, and judges of the Court of International Trade are appointed by the President with the confirmation of the Senate. The judicial branch of the government is the only one not elected by the people.

32. C: Article III judges are appointed for life and can retire at 65. They can only be removed from their posts by impeachment in the House and conviction in the Senate. Having judges serve life terms is meant to allow them to serve without being governed by the changing opinions of the public.

33. B: Judges who are eligible to retire but still work are called senior judges. Retired judges who occasionally hear cases are called recalled judges. Both senior and recalled judges handle about 15-20 percent of district and appellate court caseloads.

34. B: The appellant presents arguments in a brief that explains to the three judges on the panel why the trial court was wrong. The respondent explains why the trial court made the right decision. The appeals court usually makes the final decision, unless they send it back to trial.

35. A: A writ of certiorari is filed if a case is lost in appeals or the highest state court. The writ of certiorari is a request for the Supreme Court to hear the case, but it does not guarantee the case will be heard.

36. C: There are no formal qualifications for members of the judicial branch. However, having a background in law is an informal qualification that is considered when appointing Article III judges.

37. B: Congress has the authority to shape the judicial branch. The Supreme Court once operated with only six members. Nine has been the standard number since 1869.

38. D: Criminal cases are tried under both state law and federal law. The nature of the crime determines whether it is tried in state court or federal court.

39. C: State governments follow the example of the federal government and have executive, legislative, and judicial branches of their own, and elected governors who head the executive branch.

40. B: All states have bicameral legislatures, except Nebraska. The bicameral legislatures in states resemble the federal legislature, with an upper house and a lower house.

41. A: The 10th Amendment establishes that any power not given to the federal government in the Constitution belongs to the state and the people. The federal and local governments share many responsibilities.

42. D: Local governments are usually divided into counties and municipalities. Municipalities oversee parks and recreation services, police and fire departments, housing services, emergency medical services, municipal courts, transportation services, and public works.

43. B: Congress normally chooses the jurisdiction of federal courts. The Supreme Court has original jurisdiction in certain cases, which Congress cannot revoke. For example, the Supreme Court has the right to settle a dispute between states.

44. A: The Supreme Court interprets law and the Constitution. The inferior courts are bound to uphold the law as the Supreme Court interprets and rules on it.

45. C: The 12th Amendment passed in 1804 gave each member of the Electoral College one vote for the President and another for the Vice President. Previously, the runner-up in the Presidential election became Vice President.

46. B: Discretionary spending is dedicated to transportation, education, national resources, the environment, and international affairs. State and local governments use this money to help finance programs. Mandatory spending covers entitlements such as Medicare, Social Security, Federal Retirement, and Medicaid.

47. D: Free public education has been a U.S. tradition since the 18th century. State constitutions govern the education issues of each state, although federal, state, and local governments all work together on educational issues.

48. C: Bankruptcy cases are the jurisdiction of federal courts. It is not possible to file for bankruptcy in state or municipal courts.

49. C: Nebraska does not require voter registration, but all other states do and have their own process. State and local officials administer federal elections, and though each state has its own method for holding elections, federal elections are always held at the same time.

50. A: The citizens usually elect members of the local government such as mayors and city council. However, the state grants local governments their authority. State and local governments work independently and do not share authority the way the federal and state governments share power.

51. D: The President is the Commander-in-Chief, so the executive branch employs the Armed Forces. When members of the Armed Forces are counted, the executive branch employs over 4 million people.

52. B: The Animal and Plant Health Inspection Service, the Food and Nutrition Service, and the Forest Service are agencies in the Department of Agriculture. The Department of Agriculture ensures food safety, works with farmers, promotes trade, and protects natural resources.

53. B: The House has strict rules that limit debate. A filibuster can only occur in the Senate where Senators can speak on topics other than the bill at hand and introduce amendments. A filibuster can be ended by a supermajority vote of 60 Senators.

54. C: The Government Accountability Office was originally called the General Accounting Office and was established in 1921 to audit the budget, Congress, and the Director of the Treasury. The Government Accountability Office now oversees the effectiveness of government spending in every branch.

55. A: Arbitration between organizations or individuals takes place in civil court. Civil trials are similar to criminal proceedings and require a jury. Both parties, however, can agree to let a judge decide the case.

56. D: Washington, D.C., as the U.S. capitol, is a federal district. It has a local government in the form of a mayor and city council, but Congress has ultimate authority and can override the decisions made by the local government.

57. A: The Political Affairs Agency is part of the Department of State. The Department of State is an executive agency and the Political Affairs Agency is run by the Under Secretary who supervises the bureaus for Africa, East Asia and the Pacific, Europe and Eurasia, the Near East, South and Central Asia, the Western Hemisphere, International Organizations, and International Narcotics and Law Enforcement.

58. C: Nine Vice Presidents have succeeded as President and four of them were elected President after finishing their first term.

59. B: Every member of the Executive Cabinet has the title Secretary, but the title Attorney General is given to the head of the Justice Department.

60. B: The Senate needs a two-thirds or supermajority vote to ratify treaties. A simple majority is necessary to pass a bill or confirm the appointments of the President.

61. D: State governments are funded by sales taxes, excise taxes, license taxes, income taxes, intangible taxes, property taxes, estate taxes, and inheritance taxes. States enforce some or all of these taxes, but almost all of them utilize a sales tax. Alaska, Delaware, Montana, New Hampshire, and Oregon are the only states that do not have a sales tax.

62. A: The President has the authority to negotiate and sign treaties. Two-thirds vote of the Senate, however, is needed to ratify a treaty for it to be upheld.

63. C: State Representatives all have votes, but the five U.S. territories and the District of Columbia all have Representatives who voice opinions but are not eligible to vote on legislation.

64. C: State and federal courts issue subpoenas for court cases, and Congress has the right to subpoena experts and witnesses for congressional investigations. Failure to respond to a subpoena from either Congress or the judiciary has consequences that could include incarceration.

65. D: Federal, state, and local agencies share the responsibility of ensuring food safety. The federal government provides a small amount of funding to state programs, but state and local programs must find additional funding.

66. B: Officially titled Chief Justice of the United States, Clause 6 in Section 3 of Article I is the only time the position is mentioned: "When the President of the United States is tried, the Chief Justice shall preside."

67. A: Appellate courts simply decide if an administrative agency or trial court made a mistake that influenced the outcome of the trial. The panel of three judges does not use new evidence or testimony.

68. C: The decisions of the appellate court are usually final, but a decision can be reviewed en banc. This happens when a larger group of appeals judges reviews the decision.

69. B: The Environmental Protection Agency is not part of the Cabinet. The Environmental Protection Agency and the CIA are independent federal agencies that are part of the executive branch and are under the President's authority.

70. B: The President has the authority to grant pardons and clemencies for federal crimes, except in cases of impeachment. The House elects the Speaker of the House, the President serves two terms, and Congress declares war.

71. C: Informal qualifications are the public's expectations of Presidential candidates. These can vary, but the President is considered by many to be a moral leader. This means the public expects the President to have a strong character, so a criminal record or lapses in moral judgment can prevent a person from becoming President.

72. A: If there is a tie in the Electoral College, each state's delegation in the House of Representatives gets a vote, and the majority wins. The Senate votes on the Vice President who becomes acting President if the House does not come to a conclusion by Inauguration Day. It is possible for the Senate to tie because the former Vice President is not allowed to vote.

73. D: The Senate approves Presidential appointments and treaties. The House must also approve appointments of the Vice Presidency and any treaty involving foreign trade.

74. B: The versions of a bill that pass through both houses of Congress and are signed by the President must have the exact same wording. A conference committee brings the versions of the bill into alignment, but exact wording is rare.

75. C: There are 538 electors in the Electoral College, assigned by population. There is one for each member of the congressional delegation. The District of Columbia has three electors in the Electoral College.

76. A: Federal judges are impeached in the House and convicted in the Senate. Judges normally keep their positions for life or until they choose to retire.

77. C: Cases involving diplomats and ambassadors automatically fall under the jurisdiction of the Supreme Court.

78. B: America has a history of a two-party system dating back to the Federalist and Anti-Federalists. Different laws, culture, and a winner-take-all system make it difficult for minor parties to gain ground. America does not have a representative system where the percentage of the population that agrees with a party is represented.

79. D: Minor parties often split from major parties and take voters with them. For example, Nader's Green Party was a spoiler in the 2000 election. Gore was down by 500 votes in Florida, and Nader had 100,000 votes in that state. The influence of minor parties on elections often forces the major parties to adjust their ideology.

80. B: Special interest groups utilize e-mail and mass media. They file amicus curiae briefs in cases that do not involve them directly, and are more influential when spread throughout the nation. Special interest groups represent different sectors, but the business sector usually favors Republican candidates.

81. A: Presidential candidates are nominated at each party's national convention. The Republican and Democratic Conventions have their own processes for selecting delegates. Puerto Rico, Guam, and American Samoa are also awarded PLEO (Party Leaders and Elected Officials) delegates in the Democratic National Convention.

82. C: A caucus is a private event run by political parties, and a primary is an indirect election run by state and local governments. Voters may award delegates to candidates for the national conventions, depending on state laws.

83. B: Money given directly to a party candidate is hard money. The Federal Election Commission monitors hard money because of limitations on the amount and the money's source.

84. A: Presidential candidates are eligible for a match from the federal government (with a $250 per contribution limit) if they can privately raise $5,000 per state in twenty states. Candidates who accept public money agree to limit spending. Candidates who do not accept matching funds are free to use the money they raise privately.

85. D: Political Action Committees (PACs) raise money for political candidates and are formed by business, labor, or other special interest groups. They may donate $5,000 per candidate per election, but can contribute larger amounts for party-building activities.

86. C: Grassroots organizations are effective in campaigns. They raise money, register voters, recruit volunteers, educate voters, and communicate directly with people. Grassroots organizations do not necessarily support one of the two party platforms.

87. B: Citizens who consider themselves to be liberal are statistically single, secular, and educated. Conservatives are more likely to be married, religious, and own a firearm. Most Americans do not consider themselves to be extreme liberals or extreme conservatives.

88. A: Political socialization occurs when people are made aware of political culture, facts, and values. Family, friends, society, and the media influence political socialization. Sex, race, age, education, income, and region are also indicators of how a person will vote.

89. C: Survey sampling is used to measure public opinion on different issues such as healthcare reform, the environment, and government spending.

90. B: Female support for Democratic candidates has increased since the 1980s, and younger, college-age voters are more likely to vote Democrat. The 2008 election saw particularly strong support for Obama from women and young voters.

91. D: Democratic consensus is the term for the general agreement of the people on fundamental principles of governance and the values supporting them.

92. C: The way the media presents a candidate helps determine polls and public opinion. Candidates who the media presents favorably usually have better numbers in the polls, and candidates who are behind in the polls are often not presented favorably.

93. A: America has a history of organized political protest dating back to the American Revolution. The right to peaceful protest is protected by the First Amendment. The American labor union movement, the antislavery movement, the women's suffrage movement, and the civil rights movement all used political protest to gain support for their causes.

94. C: Surveys used to create polls find people online, conduct phone interviews, and conduct interviews face to face. Mere observation is not used to discover survey information.

95. B: Political activists usually volunteer to work for political parties, and they are chosen as electors in the Electoral College if one party carries a state in a Presidential election.

96. D: Many democratic nations have proportional representation. This type of representation awards representatives based on the number of votes each party receives. Proportional representation encourages multiple parties with focused interests.

97. B: Family, educational systems, peer groups, news, and media all influence political socialization. Adults are more likely to be influenced by their peers, news, and media.

98. A: Compassion issues such as gun control, strong environmental laws, social programs, and opposition to the death penalty show a wide gender gap, as women are more likely to support compassion issues.

99. C: Lobbyists for special interest groups petition the government. Special interest groups have been regulated because of their influence and relationships with members of Congress. PACs and special interest groups are both praised and vilified. The group Common Cause wants to end PACs.

100. B: A schema is a belief system that uses personal experiences, socialization, background, and ideological convictions to interpret a subject. A person's political affiliation is an example of a schema.

101. D: Nationalism is support and devotion to one's nation, which appeared with the development of modern nation states. The terrorist attacks of 2001 increased feeling of nationalism among U.S. citizens.

102. C: The correct answer is C. Constitutional republics provide individual rights in their Constitutions. The people elect representatives, and representatives' policies are moderated by constitutional guidelines.

103. B: Socialism was a movement spurred by the injustices of the Industrial Revolution. True socialists believe in treating all people equally and that the government should be responsible for ensuring that equality. Doing away with private property was the feeling of early communists such as Karl Marx.

104. A: The UN is a supranational institution made up of participating nations that develop international laws. Recent globalization makes supranational institutions such as the UN, EU, and ECOWAS more influential in political policies.

105. C: Authoritarian regimes closely monitor the media. Democratic systems are more open with the media. The independent media of democratic societies is allowed to report on government scandals, corruption, and unpopular policies, which would be suppressed by authoritarian regimes.

106. B: Fascism and Marxism both came out of socialism, and while they had some similarities, they did not support each other. Fascism was focused on specific nations, and Marxism focused on the working class of the world in an attempt to overthrow capitalism. Fascism sought to bring the private sector under government control while preserving private property and class divisions.

107. D: Federal, state, and local governments use laws, regulations, decisions, and actions to address public issues such as healthcare and determine public policy. Members of the private sector, religious leaders, and institutions influence public policy, but the decision lies with the government.

108. C: The process of making public policy has three stages: agenda-setting, option-formulation, and implementation. Agencies and officials meet to discuss the problem at the agenda-setting stage. Option-formulation considers different options for solving the problem and chooses the best option. Implementation is the chosen option being upheld and acted upon by the government.

109. A: The concept of mixed government dates back to antiquity. Plato and Aristotle both advocated a mixture of monarchic, aristocratic, oligarchic, and democratic governments to prevent a single class, state, or person from taking absolute power. The separation of powers in government preserves the principle of mixed government.

110. C: The President is both Head of State and Chief Executive in most countries with a Presidential system. The Parliamentary system divides them into two different positions. The Head of State is often a political figurehead, and the Prime Minister serves as the Chief Executive.

111. B: Both the President and Prime Minister can be removed from office by the legislature. The President can be impeached by Congress, and a majority of the Prime Minister's legislature can cast a "vote of no confidence."

112. D: Socialists feel that capitalism creates inequality. Many believe that nationalization is the answer to ending class distinctions and injustices, while others advocate state control within a free market economy. Corporatism does involve labor, capital, and government working together, but the private sector is not nationalized in corporatism.

113. A: A mixed economy is one that has both elements of free enterprise and the government-run programs often associated with socialism. The United States is an example of a mixed economy since citizens still have a free market, but the government controls sectors such as road repair and construction.

114. B: The International Monetary Fund (IMF) was established in 1944. The IMF works to stabilize foreign trade, reduce trade barriers, and balance trade overall. It has been compared to a credit counselor, but for developing nations. The UNDP provides initiatives and resources to help developing nations.

115. C: Direct democracy is the right of every citizen to attend meetings and vote on issues. A simple majority vote wins in a direct democracy. The logistics for direct democracy, such as holding a meeting for all state citizens, make it difficult for state and national governments to institute. Direct democracy is used on a local level in small New England towns.

116. D: Public policy covers numerous areas, and special interest groups are often associated with areas of public policy. These interest groups publish their research to influence the public policies that are chosen, such as disabilities, health, education, or human rights.

117. B: A bicameral legislature has more than one legislative house, such as an upper house and a lower house. This form of mixed government is supposed to ensure greater representation since it takes both houses to pass legislation. Many authoritarian or communist regimes have unicameral legislature, or one legislative house. Unicameral legislatures do not ensure equal representation, but they pass legislation faster than bicameral legislatures.

118. A: Nationalism legitimizes authority and establishes unity. Nationalism or secular nationalism influences world views and seeks to manage chaos. Secular nationalism has influenced the founding and formation of different governments throughout history.

119. C: A pluralist society is made up of many distinct special interest groups that represent different social minorities. These interest groups compete with each other to influence legislation. The power special interest groups exert is constantly shifting.

120. B: Most political theorists support free international trade. For example, many liberals, Marxists, social democrats, and conservatives support the idea of free international trade; however, most communist regimes have strict trade limitations.

Secret Key #1 - Time is Your Greatest Enemy

Pace Yourself

Wear a watch. At the beginning of the test, check the time (or start a chronometer on your watch to count the minutes), and check the time after every few questions to make sure you are "on schedule."

If you are forced to speed up, do it efficiently. Usually one or more answer choices can be eliminated without too much difficulty. Above all, don't panic. Don't speed up and just begin guessing at random choices. By pacing yourself, and continually monitoring your progress against your watch, you will always know exactly how far ahead or behind you are with your available time. If you find that you are one minute behind on the test, don't skip one question without spending any time on it, just to catch back up. Take 15 fewer seconds on the next four questions, and after four questions you'll have caught back up. Once you catch back up, you can continue working each problem at your normal pace.

Furthermore, don't dwell on the problems that you were rushed on. If a problem was taking up too much time and you made a hurried guess, it must be difficult. The difficult questions are the ones you are most likely to miss anyway, so it isn't a big loss. It is better to end with more time than you need than to run out of time.

Lastly, sometimes it is beneficial to slow down if you are constantly getting ahead of time. You are always more likely to catch a careless mistake by working more slowly than quickly, and among very high-scoring test takers (those who are likely to have lots of time left over), careless errors affect the score more than mastery of material.

Secret Key #2 - Guessing is not Guesswork

You probably know that guessing is a good idea - unlike other standardized tests, there is no penalty for getting a wrong answer. Even if you have no idea about a question, you still have a 20-25% chance of getting it right.

Most test takers do not understand the impact that proper guessing can have on their score. Unless you score extremely high, guessing will significantly contribute to your final score.

Monkeys Take the Test

What most test takers don't realize is that to insure that 20-25% chance, you have to guess randomly. If you put 20 monkeys in a room to take this test, assuming they answered once per question and behaved themselves, on average they would get 20-25% of the questions correct. Put 20 test takers in the room, and the average will be much lower among guessed questions. Why?

1. The test writers intentionally write deceptive answer choices that "look" right. A test taker has no idea about a question, so picks the "best looking" answer, which is often wrong. The monkey has no idea what looks good and what doesn't, so will consistently be lucky about 20-25% of the time.

2. Test takers will eliminate answer choices from the guessing pool based on a hunch or intuition. Simple but correct answers often get excluded, leaving a 0% chance of being correct. The monkey has no clue, and often gets lucky with the best choice.

This is why the process of elimination endorsed by most test courses is flawed and detrimental to your performance- test takers don't guess, they make an ignorant stab in the dark that is usually worse than random.

$5 Challenge

Let me introduce one of the most valuable ideas of this course- the $5 challenge:

You only mark your "best guess" if you are willing to bet $5 on it.
You only eliminate choices from guessing if you are willing to bet $5 on it.

Why $5? Five dollars is an amount of money that is small yet not insignificant, and can really add up fast (20 questions could cost you $100). Likewise, each answer choice on one question of the test will have a small impact on your overall score, but it can really add up to a lot of points in the end.

The process of elimination IS valuable. The following shows your chance of guessing it right:

If you eliminate wrong answer choices until only this many remain:	Chance of getting it correct:
1	100%
2	50%
3	33%

However, if you accidentally eliminate the right answer or go on a hunch for an incorrect answer, your chances drop dramatically: to 0%. By guessing among all the answer choices, you are GUARANTEED to have a shot at the right answer.

That's why the $5 test is so valuable- if you give up the advantage and safety of a pure guess, it had better be worth the risk.

What we still haven't covered is how to be sure that whatever guess you make is truly random. Here's the easiest way:

Always pick the first answer choice among those remaining.

Such a technique means that you have decided, **before you see a single test question**, exactly how you are going to guess- and since the order of choices tells you nothing about which one is correct, this guessing technique is perfectly random.

This section is not meant to scare you away from making educated guesses or eliminating choices- you just need to define when a choice is worth eliminating. The $5 test, along with a pre-defined random guessing strategy, is the best way to make sure you reap all of the benefits of guessing.

Secret Key #3 - Practice Smarter, Not Harder

Many test takers delay the test preparation process because they dread the awful amounts of practice time they think necessary to succeed on the test. We have refined an effective method that will take you only a fraction of the time.
There are a number of "obstacles" in your way to succeed. Among these are answering questions, finishing in time, and mastering test-taking strategies. All must be executed on the day of the test at peak performance, or your score will suffer. The test is a mental marathon that has a large impact on your future.

Just like a marathon runner, it is important to work your way up to the full challenge. So first you just worry about questions, and then time, and finally strategy:

Success Strategy

1. Find a good source for practice tests.
2. If you are willing to make a larger time investment, consider using more than one study guide- often the different approaches of multiple authors will help you "get" difficult concepts.
3. Take a practice test with no time constraints, with all study helps "open book." Take your time with questions and focus on applying strategies.
4. Take a practice test with time constraints, with all guides "open book."
5. Take a final practice test with no open material and time limits

If you have time to take more practice tests, just repeat step 5. By gradually exposing yourself to the full rigors of the test environment, you will condition your mind to the stress of test day and maximize your success.

Secret Key #4 - Prepare, Don't Procrastinate

Let me state an obvious fact: if you take the test three times, you will get three different scores. This is due to the way you feel on test day, the level of preparedness you have, and, despite the test writers' claims to the contrary, some tests WILL be easier for you than others.

Since your future depends so much on your score, you should maximize your chances of success. In order to maximize the likelihood of success, you've got to prepare in advance. This means taking practice tests and spending time learning the information and test taking strategies you will need to succeed.

Never take the test as a "practice" test, expecting that you can just take it again if you need to. Feel free to take sample tests on your own, but when you go to take the official test, be prepared, be focused, and do your best the first time!

Secret Key #5 - Test Yourself

Everyone knows that time is money. There is no need to spend too much of your time or too little of your time preparing for the test. You should only spend as much of your precious time preparing as is necessary for you to get the score you need.

Once you have taken a practice test under real conditions of time constraints, then you will know if you are ready for the test or not.

If you have scored extremely high the first time that you take the practice test, then there is not much point in spending countless hours studying. You are already there.

Benchmark your abilities by retaking practice tests and seeing how much you have improved. Once you score high enough to guarantee success, then you are ready.

If you have scored well below where you need, then knuckle down and begin studying in earnest. Check your improvement regularly through the use of practice tests under real conditions. Above all, don't worry, panic, or give up. The key is perseverance!

Then, when you go to take the test, remain confident and remember how well you did on the practice tests. If you can score high enough on a practice test, then you can do the same on the real thing.

General Strategies

The most important thing you can do is to ignore your fears and jump into the test immediately- do not be overwhelmed by any strange-sounding terms. You have to jump into the test like jumping into a pool- all at once is the easiest way.

Make Predictions

As you read and understand the question, try to guess what the answer will be. Remember that several of the answer choices are wrong, and once you begin reading them, your mind will immediately become cluttered with answer choices designed to throw you off. Your mind is typically the most focused immediately after you have read the question and digested its contents. If you can, try to predict what the correct answer will be. You may be surprised at what you can predict.

Quickly scan the choices and see if your prediction is in the listed answer choices. If it is, then you can be quite confident that you have the right answer. It still won't hurt to check the other answer choices, but most of the time, you've got it!

Answer the Question

It may seem obvious to only pick answer choices that answer the question, but the test writers can create some excellent answer choices that are wrong. Don't pick an answer just because it sounds right, or you believe it to be true. It MUST answer the question. Once you've made your selection, always go back and check it against the question and make sure that you didn't misread the question, and the answer choice does answer the question posed.

Benchmark

After you read the first answer choice, decide if you think it sounds correct or not. If it doesn't, move on to the next answer choice. If it does, mentally mark that answer choice. This doesn't mean that you've definitely selected it as your answer choice, it just means that it's the best you've seen thus far. Go ahead and read the next choice. If the next choice is worse than the one you've already selected, keep going to the next answer choice. If the next choice is better than the choice you've already selected, mentally mark the new answer choice as your best guess.

The first answer choice that you select becomes your standard. Every other answer choice must be benchmarked against that standard. That choice is correct until proven otherwise by another answer choice beating it out. Once you've decided that no other answer choice seems as good, do one final check to ensure that your answer choice answers the question posed.

Valid Information

Don't discount any of the information provided in the question. Every piece of information may be necessary to determine the correct answer. None of the information in the question is there to throw you off (while the answer choices will certainly have information to throw you off). If two seemingly unrelated topics are discussed, don't ignore either. You can be confident there is a relationship, or it wouldn't be included in the question, and you are probably going to have to determine what is that relationship to find the answer.

Avoid "Fact Traps"

Don't get distracted by a choice that is factually true. Your search is for the answer that answers the question. Stay focused and don't fall for an answer that is true but incorrect. Always go back to the question and make sure you're choosing an answer that actually answers the question and is not just a true statement. An answer can be factually correct, but it MUST answer the question asked. Additionally, two answers can both be seemingly correct, so be sure to read all of the answer choices, and make sure that you get the one that BEST answers the question.

Milk the Question

Some of the questions may throw you completely off. They might deal with a subject you have not been exposed to, or one that you haven't reviewed in years. While your lack of knowledge about the subject will be a hindrance, the question itself can give you many clues that will help you find the correct answer. Read the question carefully and look for clues. Watch particularly for adjectives and nouns describing difficult terms or words that you don't recognize. Regardless of if you completely understand a word or not, replacing it with a synonym either provided or one you more familiar with may help you to understand what the questions are asking. Rather than wracking your mind about specific detailed information concerning a difficult term or word, try to use mental substitutes that are easier to understand.

The Trap of Familiarity

Don't just choose a word because you recognize it. On difficult questions, you may not recognize a number of words in the answer choices. The test writers don't put "make-believe" words on the test; so don't think that just because you only recognize all the words in one answer choice means that answer choice must be correct. If you only recognize words in one answer choice, then focus on that one. Is it correct? Try your best to determine if it is correct. If it is, that is great, but if it doesn't, eliminate it. Each word and answer choice you eliminate increases your chances of getting the question correct, even if you then have to guess among the unfamiliar choices.

Eliminate Answers

Eliminate choices as soon as you realize they are wrong. But be careful! Make sure you consider all of the possible answer choices. Just because one appears right, doesn't mean that the next one won't be even better! The test writers will usually put more than one good answer choice for every question, so read all of them. Don't worry if you are stuck between two that seem right. By getting down to just two remaining possible choices, your odds are now 50/50. Rather than wasting too much time, play the odds. You are guessing, but guessing wisely, because you've been able to knock out some of the answer choices that you know are wrong. If you are eliminating choices and realize that the last answer choice you are left with is also obviously wrong, don't panic. Start over and consider each choice again. There may easily be something that you missed the first time and will realize on the second pass.

Tough Questions

If you are stumped on a problem or it appears too hard or too difficult, don't waste time. Move on! Remember though, if you can quickly check for obviously incorrect answer choices, your chances of guessing correctly are greatly improved. Before you completely give up, at least try to knock out a couple of possible answers. Eliminate what you can and then guess at the remaining answer choices before moving on.

Brainstorm

If you get stuck on a difficult question, spend a few seconds quickly brainstorming. Run through the complete list of possible answer choices. Look at each choice and ask yourself, "Could this answer the question satisfactorily?" Go through each answer choice and consider it independently of the other. By systematically going through all possibilities, you may find something that you would otherwise overlook. Remember that when you get stuck, it's important to try to keep moving.

Read Carefully

Understand the problem. Read the question and answer choices carefully. Don't miss the question because you misread the terms. You have plenty of time to read each question thoroughly and make sure you understand what is being asked. Yet a happy medium must be attained, so don't waste too much time. You must read carefully, but efficiently.

Face Value

When in doubt, use common sense. Always accept the situation in the problem at face value. Don't read too much into it. These problems will not require you to make huge leaps of logic. The test writers aren't trying to throw you off with a cheap trick. If you have to go beyond creativity and make a leap of logic in order to have an answer choice answer the question, then you should look at the other answer choices. Don't overcomplicate the problem by creating theoretical relationships or explanations that will warp time or space. These are normal problems rooted in reality. It's just that the applicable relationship or explanation may not be readily apparent and you have to figure things out. Use your common sense to interpret anything that isn't clear.

Prefixes

If you're having trouble with a word in the question or answer choices, try dissecting it. Take advantage of every clue that the word might include. Prefixes and suffixes can be a huge help. Usually they allow you to determine a basic meaning. Pre- means before, post-means after, pro - is positive, de- is negative. From these prefixes and suffixes, you can get an idea of the general meaning of the word and try to put it into context. Beware though of any traps. Just because con is the opposite of pro, doesn't necessarily mean congress is the opposite of progress!

Hedge Phrases

Watch out for critical "hedge" phrases, such as likely, may, can, will often, sometimes, often, almost, mostly, usually, generally, rarely, sometimes. Question writers insert these hedge phrases to cover every possibility. Often an answer choice will be wrong simply because it leaves no room for exception. Avoid answer choices that have definitive words like "exactly," and "always".

Switchback Words

Stay alert for "switchbacks". These are the words and phrases frequently used to alert you to shifts in thought. The most common switchback word is "but". Others include although, however, nevertheless, on the other hand, even though, while, in spite of, despite, regardless of.

New Information

Correct answer choices will rarely have completely new information included. Answer choices typically are straightforward reflections of the material asked about and will directly relate to the question. If a new piece of information is included in an answer choice that doesn't even seem to relate to the topic being asked about, then that answer choice is likely incorrect. All of the information needed to answer the question is usually provided for you, and so you should not have to make guesses that are unsupported or choose answer choices that require unknown information that cannot be reasoned on its own.

Time Management

On technical questions, don't get lost on the technical terms. Don't spend too much time on any one question. If you don't know what a term means, then since you don't have a dictionary, odds are you aren't going to get much further. You should immediately recognize terms as whether or not you know them. If you don't, work with the other clues that you have, the other answer choices and terms provided, but don't waste too much time trying to figure out a difficult term.

Contextual Clues

Look for contextual clues. An answer can be right but not correct. The contextual clues will help you find the answer that is most right and is correct. Understand the context in which a phrase or statement is made. This will help you make important distinctions.

Don't Panic

Panicking will not answer any questions for you. Therefore, it isn't helpful. When you first see the question, if your mind goes blank, take a deep breath. Force yourself to mechanically go through the steps of solving the problem and using the strategies you've learned.

Pace Yourself

Don't get clock fever. It's easy to be overwhelmed when you're looking at a page full of questions, your mind is full of random thoughts and feeling confused, and the clock is ticking down faster than you would like. Calm down and maintain the pace that you have set for yourself. As long as you are on track by monitoring your pace, you are guaranteed to have enough time for yourself. When you get to the last few minutes of the test, it may seem like you won't have enough time left, but if you only have as many questions as you should have left at that point, then you're right on track!

Answer Selection

The best way to pick an answer choice is to eliminate all of those that are wrong, until only one is left and confirm that is the correct answer. Sometimes though, an answer choice may immediately look right. Be careful! Take a second to make sure that the other choices are not equally obvious. Don't make a hasty mistake. There are only two times that you should stop before checking other answers. First is when you are positive that the answer choice you have selected is correct. Second is when time is almost out and you have to make a quick guess!

Check Your Work

Since you will probably not know every term listed and the answer to every question, it is important that you get credit for the ones that you do know. Don't miss any questions through careless mistakes. If at all possible, try to take a second to look back over your answer selection and make sure you've selected the correct answer choice and haven't made a costly careless mistake (such as marking an answer choice that you didn't mean to mark). This quick double check should more than pay for itself in caught mistakes for the time it costs.

Beware of Directly Quoted Answers

Sometimes an answer choice will repeat word for word a portion of the question or reference section. However, beware of such exact duplication – it may be a trap! More than likely, the correct choice will paraphrase or summarize a point, rather than being exactly the same wording.

Slang

Scientific sounding answers are better than slang ones. An answer choice that begins "To compare the outcomes…" is much more likely to be correct than one that begins "Because some people insisted…"

Extreme Statements

Avoid wild answers that throw out highly controversial ideas that are proclaimed as established fact. An answer choice that states the "process should be used in certain situations, if…" is much more likely to be correct than one that states the "process should be discontinued completely." The first is a calm rational statement and doesn't even make a definitive, uncompromising stance, using a hedge word "if" to provide wiggle room, whereas the second choice is a radical idea and far more extreme.

Answer Choice Families

When you have two or more answer choices that are direct opposites or parallels, one of them is usually the correct answer. For instance, if one answer choice states "x increases" and another answer choice states "x decreases" or "y increases," then those two or three answer choices are very similar in construction and fall into the same family of answer choices. A family of answer choices is when two or three answer choices are very similar in construction, and yet often have a directly opposite meaning. Usually the correct answer choice will be in that family of answer choices. The "odd man out" or answer choice that doesn't seem to fit the parallel construction of the other answer choices is more likely to be incorrect.

Special Report: What Your Test Score Will Tell You About Your IQ

Did you know that most standardized tests correlate very strongly with IQ? In fact, your general intelligence is a better predictor of your success than any other factor, and most tests intentionally measure this trait to some degree to ensure that those selected by the test are truly qualified for the test's purposes.

Before we can delve into the relation between your test score and IQ, I will first have to explain what exactly is IQ. Here's the formula:

Your IQ = 100 + (Number of standard deviations below or above the average)*15

Now, let's define standard deviations by using an example. If we have 5 people with 5 different heights, then first we calculate the average. Let's say the average was 65 inches. The standard deviation is the "average distance" away from the average of each of the members. It is a direct measure of variability - if the 5 people included Jackie Chan and Shaquille O'Neal, obviously there's a lot more variability in that group than a group of 5 sisters who are all within 6 inches in height of each other. The standard deviation uses a number to characterize the average range of difference within a group.

A convenient feature of most groups is that they have a "normal" distribution- makes sense that most things would be normal, right? Without getting into a bunch of statistical mumbo-jumbo, you just need to know that if you know the average of the group and the standard deviation, you can successfully predict someone's percentile rank in the group.

Confused? Let me give you an example. If instead of 5 people's heights, we had 100 people, we could figure out their rank in height JUST by knowing the average, standard deviation, and their height. We wouldn't need to know each person's height and manually rank them, we could just predict their rank based on three numbers.

What this means is that you can take your PERCENTILE rank that is often given with your test and relate this to your RELATIVE IQ of people taking the test - that is, your IQ relative to the people taking the test. Obviously, there's no way to know your actual IQ because the people taking a standardized test are usually not very good samples of the general population- many of those with extremely low IQ's never achieve a level of success or competency necessary to complete a typical standardized test. In fact, professional psychologists who measure IQ actually have to use non-written tests that can fairly measure the IQ of those not able to complete a traditional test.

The bottom line is to not take your test score too seriously, but it is fun to compute your "relative IQ" among the people who took the test with you. I've done the calculations below. Just look up your percentile rank in the left and then you'll see your "relative IQ" for your test in the right hand column-

Percentile	Your Relative		Percentile	Your Relative
99	135		59	103
98	131		58	103
97	128		57	103
96	126		56	102
95	125		55	102
94	123		54	102
93	122		53	101
92	121		52	101
91	120		51	100
90	119		50	100
89	118		49	100
88	118		48	99
87	117		47	99
86	116		46	98
85	116		45	98
84	115		44	98
83	114		43	97
82	114		42	97
81	113		41	97
80	113		40	96
79	112		39	96
78	112		38	95
77	111		37	95
76	111		36	95
75	110		35	94
74	110		34	94
73	109		33	93
72	109		32	93
71	108		31	93
70	108		30	92
69	107		29	92
68	107		28	91
67	107		27	91
66	106		26	90
65	106		25	90
64	105		24	89
63	105		23	89
62	105		22	88
61	104		21	88
60	104		20	87

Special Report: What is Test Anxiety and How to Overcome It?

The very nature of tests caters to some level of anxiety, nervousness or tension, just as we feel for any important event that occurs in our lives. A little bit of anxiety or nervousness can be a good thing. It helps us with motivation, and makes achievement just that much sweeter. However, too much anxiety can be a problem; especially if it hinders our ability to function and perform.

"Test anxiety," is the term that refers to the emotional reactions that some test-takers experience when faced with a test or exam. Having a fear of testing and exams is based upon a rational fear, since the test-taker's performance can shape the course of an academic career. Nevertheless, experiencing excessive fear of examinations will only interfere with the test-takers ability to perform, and his/her chances to be successful.

There are a large variety of causes that can contribute to the development and sensation of test anxiety. These include, but are not limited to lack of performance and worrying about issues surrounding the test.

Lack of Preparation

Lack of preparation can be identified by the following behaviors or situations:

Not scheduling enough time to study, and therefore cramming the night before the test or exam
Managing time poorly, to create the sensation that there is not enough time to do everything
Failing to organize the text information in advance, so that the study material consists of the entire text and not simply the pertinent information
Poor overall studying habits

Worrying, on the other hand, can be related to both the test taker, or many other factors around him/her that will be affected by the results of the test. These include worrying about:

Previous performances on similar exams, or exams in general
How friends and other students are achieving
The negative consequences that will result from a poor grade or failure

There are three primary elements to test anxiety. Physical components, which involve the same typical bodily reactions as those to acute anxiety (to be discussed below). Emotional factors have to do with fear or panic. Mental or cognitive issues concerning attention spans and memory abilities.

Physical Signals

There are many different symptoms of test anxiety, and these are not limited to mental and emotional strain. Frequently there are a range of physical signals that will let a test taker know that he/she is suffering from test anxiety. These bodily changes can include the following:

Perspiring
Sweaty palms
Wet, trembling hands
Nausea
Dry mouth
A knot in the stomach
Headache
Faintness
Muscle tension
Aching shoulders, back and neck
Rapid heart beat
Feeling too hot/cold

To recognize the sensation of test anxiety, a test-taker should monitor him/herself for the following sensations:

The physical distress symptoms as listed above
Emotional sensitivity, expressing emotional feelings such as the need to cry or laugh too much, or a sensation of anger or helplessness
A decreased ability to think, causing the test-taker to blank out or have racing thoughts that are hard to organize or control.

Though most students will feel some level of anxiety when faced with a test or exam, the majority can cope with that anxiety and maintain it at a manageable level. However, those who cannot are faced with a very real and very serious condition, which can and should be controlled for the immeasurable benefit of this sufferer.

Naturally, these sensations lead to negative results for the testing experience. The most common effects of test anxiety have to do with nervousness and mental blocking.

Nervousness

Nervousness can appear in several different levels:

The test-taker's difficulty, or even inability to read and understand the questions on the test
The difficulty or inability to organize thoughts to a coherent form
The difficulty or inability to recall key words and concepts relating to the testing questions (especially essays)
The receipt of poor grades on a test, though the test material was well known by the test taker

Conversely, a person may also experience mental blocking, which involves:

Blanking out on test questions
Only remembering the correct answers to the questions when the test has already finished.

Fortunately for test anxiety sufferers, beating these feelings, to a large degree, has to do with proper preparation. When a test taker has a feeling of preparedness, then anxiety will be dramatically lessened.

The first step to resolving anxiety issues is to distinguish which of the two types of anxiety are being suffered. If the anxiety is a direct result of a lack of preparation, this should be considered a normal reaction, and the anxiety level (as opposed to the test results) shouldn't be anything to worry about. However, if, when adequately prepared, the test-taker still panics, blanks out, or seems to overreact, this is not a fully rational reaction. While this can be considered normal too, there are many ways to combat and overcome these effects.

Remember that anxiety cannot be entirely eliminated, however, there are ways to minimize it, to make the anxiety easier to manage. Preparation is one of the best ways to minimize test anxiety. Therefore the following techniques are wise in order to best fight off any anxiety that may want to build.

To begin with, try to avoid cramming before a test, whenever it is possible. By trying to memorize an entire term's worth of information in one day, you'll be shocking your system, and not giving yourself a very good chance to absorb the information. This is an easy path to anxiety, so for those who suffer from test anxiety, cramming should not even be considered an option.

Instead of cramming, work throughout the semester to combine all of the material which is presented throughout the semester, and work on it gradually as the course goes by, making sure to master the main concepts first, leaving minor details for a week or so before the test.

To study for the upcoming exam, be sure to pose questions that may be on the examination, to gauge the ability to answer them by integrating the ideas from your texts, notes and lectures, as well as any supplementary readings.

If it is truly impossible to cover all of the information that was covered in that particular term, concentrate on the most important portions, that can be covered very well. Learn these concepts as best as possible, so that when the test comes, a goal can be made to use these concepts as presentations of your knowledge.

In addition to study habits, changes in attitude are critical to beating a struggle with test anxiety. In fact, an improvement of the perspective over the entire test-taking experience can actually help a test taker to enjoy studying and therefore improve the overall experience. Be certain not to overemphasize the significance of the grade - know that the result of the test is neither a reflection of self worth, nor is it a measure of intelligence; one grade will not predict a person's future success.

To improve an overall testing outlook, the following steps should be tried:

Keeping in mind that the most reasonable expectation for taking a test is to expect to try to demonstrate as much of what you know as you possibly can.
Reminding ourselves that a test is only one test; this is not the only one, and there will be others.
The thought of thinking of oneself in an irrational, all-or-nothing term should be avoided at all costs.
A reward should be designated for after the test, so there's something to look forward to. Whether it be going to a movie, going out to eat, or simply visiting friends, schedule it in advance, and do it no matter what result is expected on the exam.

Test-takers should also keep in mind that the basics are some of the most important things, even beyond anti-anxiety techniques and studying. Never neglect the basic social, emotional and biological needs, in order to try to absorb information. In order to best achieve, these three factors must be held as just as important as the studying itself.

Study Steps

Remember the following important steps for studying:

Maintain healthy nutrition and exercise habits. Continue both your recreational activities and social pass times. These both contribute to your physical and emotional well being.
Be certain to get a good amount of sleep, especially the night before the test, because when you're overtired you are not able to perform to the best of your best ability.
Keep the studying pace to a moderate level by taking breaks when they are needed, and varying the work whenever possible, to keep the mind fresh instead of getting bored.
When enough studying has been done that all the material that can be learned has been learned, and the test taker is prepared for the test, stop studying and do something relaxing such as listening to music, watching a movie, or taking a warm bubble bath.

There are also many other techniques to minimize the uneasiness or apprehension that is experienced along with test anxiety before, during, or even after the examination. In fact, there are a great deal of things that can be done to stop anxiety from interfering with lifestyle and performance. Again, remember that anxiety will not be eliminated entirely, and it shouldn't be. Otherwise that "up" feeling for exams would not exist, and most of us depend on that sensation to perform better than usual. However, this anxiety has to be at a level that is manageable.

Of course, as we have just discussed, being prepared for the exam is half the battle right away. Attending all classes, finding out what knowledge will be expected on the exam, and knowing the exam schedules are easy steps to lowering anxiety. Keeping up with work will remove the need to cram, and efficient study habits will eliminate wasted time. Studying should be done in an ideal location for concentration, so that it is simple to become interested in the material and give it complete attention. A method such as SQ3R (Survey, Question, Read, Recite, Review) is a wonderful key to follow to make sure that the study habits are as effective as possible, especially in the case of learning from a textbook. Flashcards are great techniques for memorization. Learning to take good notes will mean that notes will be full of useful information, so that less sifting will need to be done to seek out what is pertinent for studying. Reviewing notes after class and then again on occasion will keep the information fresh in the mind. From notes that have been taken summary sheets and outlines can be made for simpler reviewing.

A study group can also be a very motivational and helpful place to study, as there will be a sharing of ideas, all of the minds can work together, to make sure that everyone understands, and the studying will be made more interesting because it will be a social occasion.

Basically, though, as long as the test-taker remains organized and self confident, with efficient study habits, less time will need to be spent studying, and higher grades will be achieved.

To become self confident, there are many useful steps. The first of these is "self talk." It has been shown through extensive research, that self-talk for students who suffer from test anxiety, should be well monitored, in order to make sure that it contributes to self confidence as opposed to sinking the student. Frequently the self talk of test-anxious students is negative or self-defeating, thinking that everyone else is smarter and faster, that they always mess up, and that if they don't do well, they'll fail the entire course. It is important to decreasing anxiety that awareness is made of self talk. Try writing any negative self thoughts and then disputing them with a positive statement instead. Begin self-encouragement as though it was a friend speaking. Repeat positive statements to help reprogram the mind to believing in successes instead of failures.

Helpful Techniques

Other extremely helpful techniques include:

Self-visualization of doing well and reaching goals
While aiming for an "A" level of understanding, don't try to "overprotect" by setting your expectations lower. This will only convince the mind to stop studying in order to meet the lower expectations.
Don't make comparisons with the results or habits of other students. These are individual factors, and different things work for different people, causing different results.
Strive to become an expert in learning what works well, and what can be done in order to improve. Consider collecting this data in a journal.
Create rewards for after studying instead of doing things before studying that will only turn into avoidance behaviors.
Make a practice of relaxing - by using methods such as progressive relaxation, self-hypnosis, guided imagery, etc - in order to make relaxation an automatic sensation.
Work on creating a state of relaxed concentration so that concentrating will take on the focus of the mind, so that none will be wasted on worrying.
Take good care of the physical self by eating well and getting enough sleep.
Plan in time for exercise and stick to this plan.

Beyond these techniques, there are other methods to be used before, during and after the test that will help the test-taker perform well in addition to overcoming anxiety.

Before the exam comes the academic preparation. This involves establishing a study schedule and beginning at least one week before the actual date of the test. By doing this, the anxiety of not having enough time to study for the test will be automatically eliminated. Moreover, this will make the studying a much more effective experience, ensuring that the learning will be an easier process. This relieves much undue pressure on the test-taker.

Summary sheets, note cards, and flash cards with the main concepts and examples of these main concepts should be prepared in advance of the actual studying time. A topic should never be eliminated from this process. By omitting a topic because it isn't expected to be on the test is only setting up the test-taker for anxiety should it actually appear on the exam. Utilize the course syllabus for laying out the topics that should be studied. Carefully go over the notes that were made in class, paying special attention to any of the issues that the professor took special care to emphasize while lecturing in class. In the textbooks, use the chapter review, or if possible, the chapter tests, to begin your review.

It may even be possible to ask the instructor what information will be covered on the exam, or what the format of the exam will be (for example, multiple choice, essay, free form, true-false). Additionally, see if it is possible to find out how many questions will be on the test. If a review sheet or sample test has been offered by the professor, make good use of it, above anything else, for the preparation for the test. Another great resource for getting to know the examination is reviewing tests from previous semesters. Use these tests to review, and aim to achieve a 100% score on each of the possible topics. With a few exceptions, the goal that you set for yourself is the highest one that you will reach.

Take all of the questions that were assigned as homework, and rework them to any other possible course material. The more problems reworked, the more skill and confidence will form as a result. When forming the solution to a problem, write out each of the steps. Don't simply do head work. By doing as many steps on paper as possible, much clarification and therefore confidence will be formed. Do this with as many homework problems as possible, before checking the answers. By checking the answer after each problem, a reinforcement will exist, that will not be on the exam. Study situations should be as exam-like as possible, to prime the test-taker's system for the experience. By waiting to check the answers at the end, a psychological advantage will be formed, to decrease the stress factor.

Another fantastic reason for not cramming is the avoidance of confusion in concepts, especially when it comes to mathematics. 8-10 hours of study will become one hundred percent more effective if it is spread out over a week or at least several days, instead of doing it all in one sitting. Recognize that the human brain requires time in order to assimilate new material, so frequent breaks and a span of study time over several days will be much more beneficial.

Additionally, don't study right up until the point of the exam. Studying should stop a minimum of one hour before the exam begins. This allows the brain to rest and put things in their proper order. This will also provide the time to become as relaxed as possible when going into the examination room. The test-taker will also have time to eat well and eat sensibly. Know that the brain needs food as much as the rest of the body. With enough food and enough sleep, as well as a relaxed attitude, the body and the mind are primed for success.

Avoid any anxious classmates who are talking about the exam. These students only spread anxiety, and are not worth sharing the anxious sentimentalities.

Before the test also involves creating a positive attitude, so mental preparation should also be a point of concentration. There are many keys to creating a positive attitude. Should fears become rushing in, make a visualization of taking the exam, doing well, and seeing an A written on the paper. Write out a list of affirmations that will bring a feeling of confidence, such as "I am doing well in my English class," "I studied well and know my material," "I enjoy this class." Even if the affirmations aren't believed at first, it sends a positive message to the subconscious which will result in an alteration of the overall belief system, which is the system that creates reality.

If a sensation of panic begins, work with the fear and imagine the very worst! Work through the entire scenario of not passing the test, failing the entire course, and dropping out of school, followed by not getting a job, and pushing a shopping cart through the dark alley where you'll live. This will place things into perspective! Then, practice deep breathing and create a visualization of the opposite situation - achieving an "A" on the exam, passing the entire course, receiving the degree at a graduation ceremony.

On the day of the test, there are many things to be done to ensure the best results, as well as the most calm outlook. The following stages are suggested in order to maximize test-taking potential:

Begin the examination day with a moderate breakfast, and avoid any coffee or beverages with caffeine if the test taker is prone to jitters. Even people who are used to managing caffeine can feel jittery or light-headed when it is taken on a test day.

Attempt to do something that is relaxing before the examination begins. As last minute cramming clouds the mastering of overall concepts, it is better to use this time to create a calming outlook.

Be certain to arrive at the test location well in advance, in order to provide time to select a location that is away from doors, windows and other distractions, as well as giving enough time to relax before the test begins.

Keep away from anxiety generating classmates who will upset the sensation of stability and relaxation that is being attempted before the exam.

Should the waiting period before the exam begins cause anxiety, create a self-distraction by reading a light magazine or something else that is relaxing and simple.

During the exam itself, read the entire exam from beginning to end, and find out how much time should be allotted to each individual problem. Once writing the exam, should more time be taken for a problem, it should be abandoned, in order to begin another problem. If there is time at the end, the unfinished problem can always be returned to and completed.

Read the instructions very carefully - twice - so that unpleasant surprises won't follow during or after the exam has ended.

When writing the exam, pretend that the situation is actually simply the completion of homework within a library, or at home. This will assist in forming a relaxed atmosphere, and will allow the brain extra focus for the complex thinking function.

Begin the exam with all of the questions with which the most confidence is felt. This will build the confidence level regarding the entire exam and will begin a quality momentum. This will also create encouragement for trying the problems where uncertainty resides.

Going with the "gut instinct" is always the way to go when solving a problem. Second guessing should be avoided at all costs. Have confidence in the ability to do well.

For essay questions, create an outline in advance that will keep the mind organized and make certain that all of the points are remembered. For multiple choice, read every answer, even if the correct one has been spotted - a better one may exist.

Continue at a pace that is reasonable and not rushed, in order to be able to work carefully. Provide enough time to go over the answers at the end, to check for small errors that can be corrected.

Should a feeling of panic begin, breathe deeply, and think of the feeling of the body releasing sand through its pores. Visualize a calm, peaceful place, and include all of the sights, sounds and sensations of this image. Continue the deep breathing, and take a few minutes to continue this with closed eyes. When all is well again, return to the test.

If a "blanking" occurs for a certain question, skip it and move on to the next question. There will be time to return to the other question later. Get everything done that can be done, first, to guarantee all the grades that can be compiled, and to build all of the confidence possible. Then return to the weaker questions to build the marks from there.

Remember, one's own reality can be created, so as long as the belief is there, success will follow. And remember: anxiety can happen later, right now, there's an exam to be written!

After the examination is complete, whether there is a feeling for a good grade or a bad grade, don't dwell on the exam, and be certain to follow through on the reward that was promised...and enjoy it! Don't dwell on any mistakes that have been made, as there is nothing that can be done at this point anyway.

Additionally, don't begin to study for the next test right away. Do something relaxing for a while, and let the mind relax and prepare itself to begin absorbing information again.

From the results of the exam - both the grade and the entire experience, be certain to learn from what has gone on. Perfect studying habits and work some more on confidence in order to make the next examination experience even better than the last one.

Learn to avoid places where openings occurred for laziness, procrastination and day dreaming.

Use the time between this exam and the next one to better learn to relax, even learning to relax on cue, so that any anxiety can be controlled during the next exam. Learn how to relax the body. Slouch in your chair if that helps. Tighten and then relax all of the different muscle groups, one group at a time, beginning with the feet and then working all the way up to the neck and face. This will ultimately relax the muscles more than they were to begin with. Learn how to breathe deeply and comfortably, and focus on this breathing going in and out as a relaxing thought. With every exhale, repeat the word "relax."

As common as test anxiety is, it is very possible to overcome it. Make yourself one of the test-takers who overcome this frustrating hindrance.

Special Report: Retaking the Test: What Are Your Chances at Improving Your Score?

After going through the experience of taking a major test, many test takers feel that once is enough. The test usually comes during a period of transition in the test taker's life, and taking the test is only one of a series of important events. With so many distractions and conflicting recommendations, it may be difficult for a test taker to rationally determine whether or not he should retake the test after viewing his scores.

The importance of the test usually only adds to the burden of the retake decision. However, don't be swayed by emotion. There a few simple questions that you can ask yourself to guide you as you try to determine whether a retake would improve your score:

1. What went wrong? Why wasn't your score what you expected?

Can you point to a single factor or problem that you feel caused the low score? Were you sick on test day? Was there an emotional upheaval in your life that caused a distraction? Were you late for the test or not able to use the full time allotment? If you can point to any of these specific, individual problems, then a retake should definitely be considered.

2. Is there enough time to improve?

Many problems that may show up in your score report may take a lot of time for improvement. A deficiency in a particular math skill may require weeks or months of tutoring and studying to improve. If you have enough time to improve an identified weakness, then a retake should definitely be considered.

3. How will additional scores be used? Will a score average, highest score, or most recent score be used?

Different test scores may be handled completely differently. If you've taken the test multiple times, sometimes your highest score is used, sometimes your average score is computed and used, and sometimes your most recent score is used. Make sure you understand what method will be used to evaluate your scores, and use that to help you determine whether a retake should be considered.

4. Are my practice test scores significantly higher than my actual test score?

If you have taken a lot of practice tests and are consistently scoring at a much higher level than your actual test score, then you should consider a retake. However, if you've taken five practice tests and only one of your scores was higher than your actual test score, or if your practice test scores were only slightly higher than your actual test score, then it is unlikely that you will significantly increase your score.

5. Do I need perfect scores or will I be able to live with this score? Will this score still allow me to follow my dreams?

What kind of score is acceptable to you? Is your current score "good enough?" Do you have to have a certain score in order to pursue the future of your dreams? If you won't be happy with your current score, and there's no way that you could live with it, then you should consider a retake. However, don't get your hopes up. If you are looking for significant improvement, that may or may not be possible. But if you won't be happy otherwise, it is at least worth the effort.

Remember that there are other considerations. To achieve your dream, it is likely that your grades may also be taken into account. A great test score is usually not the only thing necessary to succeed. Make sure that you aren't overemphasizing the importance of a high test score.

Furthermore, a retake does not always result in a higher score. Some test takers will score lower on a retake, rather than higher. One study shows that one-fourth of test takers will achieve a significant improvement in test score, while one-sixth of test takers will actually show a decrease. While this shows that most test takers will improve, the majority will only improve their scores a little and a retake may not be worth the test taker's effort.

Finally, if a test is taken only once and is considered in the added context of good grades on the part of a test taker, the person reviewing the grades and scores may be tempted to assume that the test taker just had a bad day while taking the test, and may discount the low test score in favor of the high grades. But if the test is retaken and the scores are approximately the same, then the validity of the low scores are only confirmed. Therefore, a retake could actually hurt a test taker by definitely bracketing a test taker's score ability to a limited range.